Practical
Linear Algebra
Principles & Software

by **D. James Benton**
software available free online

Preface

Linear algebra, that is, the manipulation and solution of simultaneous linear equations, forms the core of many problems, from curve fitting to computational fluid dynamics. Efficient and accurate assembly and processing of these relationships is essential to effectively implementing diverse mathematical tasks. In this text we will examine the many types, characteristics, methods, and means of dealing with these systems of equations. Topics covered in this text will range from sparse matrices to vectorization to singular value decomposition. All of the software is available free online.

All of the examples contained in this book,
(as well as a lot of free programs) are available at...

https://www.dudleybenton.altervista.org/software/index.html

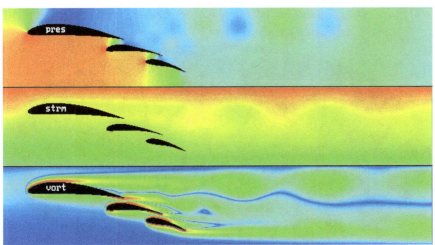

Figure 1. Turbulent Flow over 3 Airfoils

The program used to create this figure (NAST2D) uses a simple grid of evenly-spaced nodes. Arrangement of the variables in memory simplifies addressing and minimizes matrix operations, allowing complex problems to be solved with minimal resources—much more efficiently than codes that do not follow this approach.

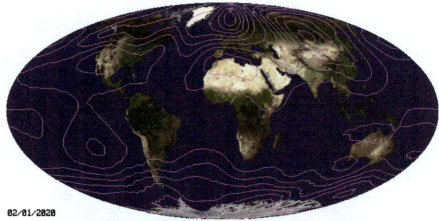

02/01/2020

Figure 2. Global Barometric Pressure Contours

These were found by solving Laplace's Equation using data from NOAA.
(Algorithms to solve this partial differential equation are discussed in this text.)

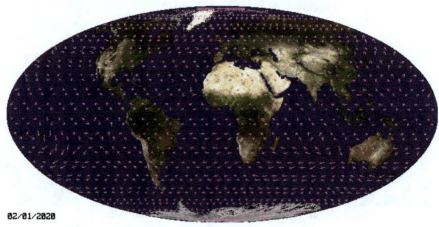

02/01/2020

Figure 3. Global Wind Vectors

These were found by taking the gradient (a vector operation we
discuss in this text) of the global barometric pressure shown above.

ii

Table of Contents

page

Preface i
Chapter 1. Introduction 1
Chapter 2. Vectors 3
Chapter 3. Vectors as Matrices 7
Chapter 4. Direct Matrix Solutions 9
Chapter 5. Direct Matrix Inversion 11
Chapter 6. Matrix Determinant 13
Chapter 7. Lagrange Multipliers 15
Chapter 8. Vandermomde 19
Chapter 8. Simple Iterative Solutions 21
Chapter 9. Conjugate-Gradient Method 25
Chapter 10. Singular Value Decomposition of a Matrix 29
Chapter 11. Potential to Gradient 33
Chapter 12. Vectorizable Methods 41
Chapter 13. Animations, 3D Rendering, and Color Depth 43
Chapter 14. Inviscid Flow Example 53
Chapter 15. Steady-State 2D Conduction Using FEM 57
Chapter 16. Plane Stress and Strain Using FEM 65
Chapter 17. An Example with History 75
Chapter 18. NAST2D 85
Appendix A. Simple Matrix Operation Code 89
Appendix B. Accelerated Vector Instructions 95
Appendix C. Burkardt's Eispack 97
Appendix D. EFDC Solvers 99

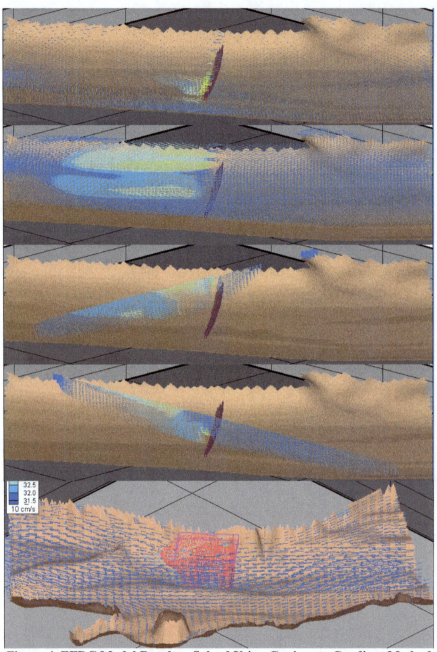

Figure 4. EFDC Model Results - Solved Using Conjugate-Gradient Method

Chapter 1. Introduction

Perhaps the simplest definition of a linear equation is a relationship between two variables that plots a straight line. Systems of linear equations and their solution extend back in time to antiquity, with the ancient Chinese, Greek, and Arabic mathematical texts. Formal treatment of the subject began in Europe with the introduction in 1637 by Descartes[1] of coordinates in geometry. Cartesian geometry and coordinates derive their name from the first descriptor. In this context (*Cartesian Geometry*), lines and planes are represented by linear equations, and computing their intersections involves solving systems of linear equations.

The first systematic methods for solving linear systems used determinants, first described by Leibniz[2] in 1693 and later Cramer[3] in 1750, from which we get *Cramer's Rule*. Gauss[4] further developed the method of elimination, which was initially listed as an advancement in geodesy. The procedure for solving simultaneous linear equations is now called *Gaussian Elimination*, also known as row reduction.

Using row operations to convert a matrix into reduced row echelon form is sometimes called Gauss–Jordan elimination. Some authors use the term Gaussian elimination to refer to the process until it has reached its upper triangular, or (unreduced) row echelon form. For computational reasons, when solving systems of linear equations, it is sometimes preferable to stop row operations before the matrix is completely reduced.

Some methods and algorithms work well for some matrices but not for others. This disparity arises from several sources, ultimately the individual values and their relation to each other. In order to effectively solve problems, we must know why this happens, how to recognize it, and what to do about it. This is why there are multiple approaches to solving what on the surface appears to be the same problem. Some algorithms are faster than others, but the fastest ones may not be the most robust. We will consider these things.

---

[1] René Descartes (1596–1650) French philosopher, mathematician, and scientist.
[2] Gottfried Wilhelm von Leibniz (1646-1716) German logician, mathematician and natural philosopher.
[3] Gabriel Cramer (1704–1752) Swiss mathematician known for contributions to linear algebra.
[4] Johann Carl Friedrich Gauss (1777–1855) German mathematician and physicist who made significant contributions to diverse fields of study.

1

Many important problems are nonlinear. Solution techniques that work for linear problems can sometimes be modified to also work on nonlinear ones. Again, sometimes these may work and sometimes not. We will compare several such methods so that understanding of *linear* algebra is essential for attacking *nonlinear* problems as well. The notation, logic, and programming are common to both.

Chapter 2. Vectors

The terminology and rules surrounding linear algebra arise from vectors and so we begin here. While we often associate vectors with three-dimensional space, they can be quite useful in a wide variety of applications from engineering to economics to medicine and span many more than three dimensions. Consider the following familiar figure:

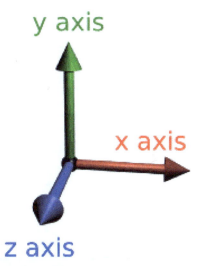

Figure 5. Three-Dimensions of Space as Vectors

In this context we often refer to three unit vectors: $\hat{i}$, $\hat{j}$, and $\hat{K}$. These have unit length (i.e., value of one) and lie on the **x**, **y**, and **z** axes, respectively. These serve to introduce and illustrate two foundational concepts of vector products. First is the *scalar* product, designated by a dot (•). Unlike a vector, a scalar has no direction, only a value. The scalar (or dot) product of any two vectors is always a scalar. Dot products of these three unit vectors reveal an important relationship: $\hat{i}•\hat{j}=0$, $\hat{i}•\hat{K}=0$, and $\hat{j}•\hat{K}=0$. The dot product of any two perpendicular vectors is zero. Another way of expressing the dot product of two vectors is given by the following equation:

$$\vec{a} \cdot \vec{b} = |a||b|\cos(\theta) \qquad (2.1)$$

or the vector **a** dot the vector **b** is equal to the length of **a** times the length of **b** times the cosine of the angle between the two, θ. If the angle, θ, is 90 then the cosine is zero and we say that the two are perpendicular. This holds for any two vectors, as shown in this next figure:

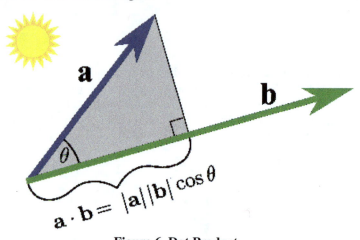

Figure 6. Dot Product

Another way of looking at the dot product is the projection (or shadow) of one vector onto another. Two perpendicular vectors cast no shadow upon each other so that their dot product is zero.

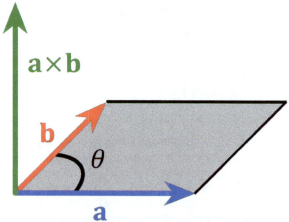

Figure 7. Cross Product

The second foundational concept is the cross (or vector) product, designated by the times symbol (×). The cross product of two vectors is also a vector. Considering these same products, only cross rather than dot, we get: $\hat{i}×\hat{j}=\hat{k}$, $\hat{j}×\hat{k}=\hat{i}$, and $\hat{k}×\hat{i}=\hat{j}$. The cross product can be expressed by the following equation:

$$\vec{a}×\vec{b} = |a||b|\sin(\theta)\hat{n} \qquad (2.2)$$

4

where θ is the angle between the two vectors (in the plane that contains both) and $\hat{n}$ is the unit vector in the direction perpendicular to the plane that contains both vectors **a** and **b**. The magnitude of the resulting vector (**a**×**b**) is equal to the shaded area in the figure above. If the vectors collapse on top of each other (i.e., $\theta=0$) then the sine is zero in contrast to the dot product, which is calculated using the cosine.

The orientation (direction or sign) of the three sequential cross products of the three unit vectors above is governed by the right-hand thumb rule, as illustrated in this next figure:

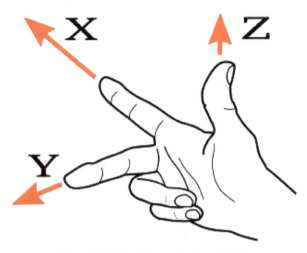

Figure 8. Right-Hand Thumb Rule

This is admittedly a preference and not a mathematical conclusion, as we might just as well have a left-hand thumb rule. What matters is that we apply it consistently. Sometimes this "rule" is described thus: point the fingers on your right hand in the direction of the first vector, then curl them toward the second vector, whereupon your right thumb will be pointing in the direction of the third vector.

Before we move on from vectors, we introduce the concept of vector addition. To accomplish this, we put the tail of the second vector at the head of the first vector and draw a line from the tail of the first vector to the head of the second to get the resultant, as shown in this next figure:

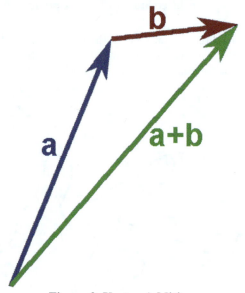

Figure 9. Vector Addition

Chapter 3. Vectors as Matrices

Vectors can naturally be represented in matrix form, as can the associated operations. For example, the following shows the addition of two 3x1 vectors:

$$\begin{vmatrix} a \\ b \\ c \end{vmatrix} + \begin{vmatrix} x \\ y \\ z \end{vmatrix} = \begin{vmatrix} a+x \\ b+y \\ c+z \end{vmatrix} \tag{3.1}$$

The scalar (dot) product of the same two vectors is shown below:

$$\begin{vmatrix} a & b & c \end{vmatrix} \times \begin{vmatrix} x \\ y \\ z \end{vmatrix} = \begin{vmatrix} ax+by+cz \end{vmatrix} \tag{3.2}$$

This representation of the dot product illustrates the fact that we must have the same number of rows in the first matrix as columns in the second. If the first were $P=[a,b,c]$ and the second $Q=[x,y,z]$ we would write this operation: P^TQ, where the superscript T indicates the transpose. The dot product is simply the multiplication of two column matrices. We can easily accomplish this with a bit of code. For the general case of matrix multiplication, we represent three matrices (P, Q, and R) as pointers to arrays; that is, the address in memory of the first element. In this case the size of P and Q are 3x1 (or 1x3 doesn't matter in this case) and R is 1x1. The dimensions are l, m, and n, where P has dimension [lxm], Q has dimension [mxn], and R has dimension [lxn]. The C code is then:

```
void MatrixMultiply(double*P,double*Q,double*R,int l,
   int m,int n)
   {
   int i,j,k;
   for(i=0;i<l;i++)
     for(k=0;k<n;k++)
       for(R[n*i+k]=j=0;j<m;j++)
         R[n*i+k]+=P[m*i+j]*Q[n*j+k];
   }
```

We can use these same few lines of C to multiply matrices of any size. For more simple matrix codes see Appendix A. For very large arrays it may be advantageous to use special instructions, as discussed in Appendix B.

7

The outer product (instead of inner product) of 3.2 can be represented:

$$
\begin{bmatrix} a \\ b \\ c \end{bmatrix} \times \begin{bmatrix} x & y & z \end{bmatrix} = \begin{bmatrix} ax & ay & az \\ bx & by & bz \\ cx & cy & cz \end{bmatrix} \tag{3.3}
$$

Note here we have a 3x1 times a 1x3 resulting in a 3x3 matrix.

Chapter 4. Direct Matrix Solutions

Let us begin with how simultaneous linear equations and their solution is introduced in algebra. Consider this set of three equations:

$$2x + 2y - 2z = 8$$
$$4x + 2y + 2z = 18 \qquad (4.1)$$
$$x - y + z = 2$$

We first eliminate x in the second row by subtracting twice the first row and eliminate x in the third row by subtracting half the first row:

$$2x + 2y - 2z = 8$$
$$0x - 2y + 6z = 2 \qquad (4.2)$$
$$0x - 2y + 2z = -2$$

Then we eliminate y from the third row by subtracting the second row:

$$2x + 2y - 2z = 8$$
$$0x - 2y + 6z = 2 \qquad (4.3)$$
$$0x + 0y - 4z = -4$$

From the third equation we get z=1. Back-solving the second equation we get y=2. Back-solving the first equation we get x=3.

$$x = 3$$
$$y = 2 \qquad (4.4)$$
$$z = 1$$

If we left out (implied) the variables (x, y, z) and simply worked with the numbers, this process of row elimination becomes Gauss' method. If we worked back up from the bottom eliminating from the left, leaving a diagonal matrix:

$$2x + 0y + 0z = 6$$
$$0x - 2y + 0z = -4 \qquad (4.5)$$
$$0x + 0y - 4z = -4$$

we have Gauss-Jordan elimination, which is the most common approach to solving simultaneous linear equations.

9

Most often we represent this problem as **AX=B**, or:

$$[A] \times [X] = [B] \qquad (4.6)$$

which for 3x3 expands to:

$$\begin{bmatrix} A_{11} & A_{12} & A_{13} \\ A_{21} & A_{22} & A_{23} \\ A_{31} & A_{32} & A_{33} \end{bmatrix} \times \begin{bmatrix} X_1 \\ X_2 \\ X_3 \end{bmatrix} = \begin{bmatrix} B_1 \\ B_2 \\ B_3 \end{bmatrix} \qquad (4.7)$$

Row Pivoting

When implementing the Gauss-Jordan elimination algorithm it is necessary to add what is called, *row pivoting*. Sometimes when we subtract a row to eliminate a variable, two on the same row become zero. This would leave a zero on the diagonal, which would result in a divide-by-zero during the back-solve phase. We can usually fix this by rearranging (swapping) the rows at the bottom. If no rearrangement eliminates the zero on the diagonal, then the matrix is not solvable—a condition we refer to as, *singular*. The order in which we solve the equations (shown by example in Equation 4.1) is immaterial; therefore, there are no additional calculations required by row pivoting or swapping rows.

Column Pivoting

Conceptually, *column pivoting* (swapping columns) should be unnecessary. In an ideal world, perhaps working with integers and not finite precision floating-point numbers, this might be true; but that's not the world we live in. What's called *round-off error* can make a matrix appear singular or yield solutions far from the true values. While there have been some attempts to develop a theoretical proof that column pivoting often produces more accurate results, this goal has proven elusive. It is, however, easy to demonstrate by example that this is often the case.

The prevailing strategy is to use row and column pivoting to move the largest (absolute value) element in the matrix into the current diagonal position and use this to eliminate (or reduce) the rows below. While row pivoting doesn't require any other action, column pivoting does; therefore, you must keep track of the column pivots and "un-pivot" the final result in order to obtain the correct solution. This requires allocating a temporary array to contain the pivot indices. A brief code to implement Gauss-Jordan elimination with row and column pivoting may be found in Appendix A.

Chapter 5. Direct Matrix Inversion

We often want to invert a matrix, which is like finding the inverse of a number, if this were a 1x1 problem. We designate the matrix inverse by the superscript or exponent −1, as in $A^{-1}B=X$. Equation 4.6 becomes:

$$[A]^{-1} \times [B] = [X] \tag{5.1}$$

The Gauss-Jordan reduction algorithm can also be used to invert a matrix. For this we extend the matrix **A** by adding the identity matrix, **I**, off to the right. The identity matrix has all zeroes except for the diagonal elements, which are all one.

$$\begin{vmatrix} A_{11} & A_{12} & A_{13} \\ A_{21} & A_{22} & A_{23} \\ A_{31} & A_{32} & A_{33} \end{vmatrix} \begin{vmatrix} 1 & 0 & 0 \\ 0 & 1 & 0 \\ 0 & 0 & 1 \end{vmatrix} \tag{5.2}$$

We first reduce the left side to an upper triangular matrix (all zeroes below the diagonal), then continue on backwards to make all the elements above the diagonal zero. When we're done, the left side (that was **A**) will be the identity matrix and the right side will be the inverse, A^{-1}. The inverse of the matrix in 4.1 is:

$$\begin{bmatrix} 2 & 2 & -2 \\ 4 & 2 & 2 \\ 1 & -1 & 1 \end{bmatrix}^{-1} = \begin{bmatrix} 0.25 & 0.0 & 0.5 \\ -0.125 & 0.25 & -0.75 \\ -0.375 & 0.25 & -0.25 \end{bmatrix} \tag{5.3}$$

Excel™ has a built-in function to invert a matrix called MINVERSE. There are also functions to multiply a matrix (MMULT) and find the transpose (TRANSPOSE). You can solve a matrix with Excel using MINVERSE and MMULT or you can set up the LINEST function to accomplish the same thing.

$$\begin{bmatrix} 2 & 2 & -2 \\ 4 & 2 & 2 \\ 1 & -1 & 1 \end{bmatrix} \begin{bmatrix} 8 \\ 18 \\ 2 \end{bmatrix} \begin{bmatrix} 1 \\ 2 \\ 3 \end{bmatrix} \tag{5.4}$$

Here we arranged [A] and [B] and used LINEST to calculate [X]. The code to accomplish this [=TRANSPOSE(LINEST(E1:E3,A1:C3,FALSE,FALSE))] is shown in this next figure:

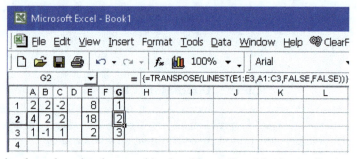

A simple code to implement this algorithm is listed in Appendix A.

Chapter 6. Matrix Determinant

Sometimes when presenting the solution of simultaneous linear equations the topic of determinants is also covered. It may also have been explained that if you swap the solution vector **[B]** with one of the columns in **[A]** and divide the determinant of the modified matrix by the determinant of the original, you will arrive at that element of the solution. Excel™ also has a built-in function to calculate the determinant (MDETERM) that we can use to illustrate this. The symbolic representation of the determinant is basically the same as the absolute value (∥) although the determinant can be negative. From the example in Chapter 4 we see:

$$\frac{\begin{vmatrix} 8 & 2 & -2 \\ 18 & 2 & 2 \\ 2 & -1 & 1 \end{vmatrix}}{\begin{vmatrix} 2 & 2 & -2 \\ 4 & 2 & 2 \\ 1 & -1 & 1 \end{vmatrix}} = \frac{48}{16} = 3 \tag{6.1}$$

$$\frac{\begin{vmatrix} 2 & 8 & -2 \\ 4 & 18 & 2 \\ 1 & 2 & 1 \end{vmatrix}}{\begin{vmatrix} 2 & 2 & -2 \\ 4 & 2 & 2 \\ 1 & -1 & 1 \end{vmatrix}} = \frac{32}{16} = 2 \tag{6.2}$$

$$\frac{\begin{vmatrix} 2 & 2 & 8 \\ 4 & 2 & 18 \\ 1 & -1 & 2 \end{vmatrix}}{\begin{vmatrix} 2 & 2 & -2 \\ 4 & 2 & 2 \\ 1 & -1 & 1 \end{vmatrix}} = \frac{16}{16} = 1 \qquad (6.3)$$

We can also see from this that if the determinant of the original matrix is zero, the solution does not exist, as we would divide by zero (hence the term *singular matrix*). This is just one use of the determinant and so we consider how this value can be calculated. The determinant of a 1x1 matrix is simply that. In Algebra 1 class we might have seen the determinant of a 2x2 matrix:

$$\begin{vmatrix} a & b \\ c & d \end{vmatrix} = ad - bc \qquad (6.4)$$

The determinant of a 3x3 matrix is:

$$\begin{vmatrix} a & b & c \\ d & e & f \\ g & h & i \end{vmatrix} = \begin{array}{l} aei + bfg + cdh \\ -ceg - bdi - afh \end{array} \qquad (6.5)$$

We can sequentially reduce the size of the matrix and calculate the determinant of each cluster of 2x2 elements, eventually arriving at the determinant. This approach is attributed to Leibniz. This method may be useful in classroom instruction and from an historical perspective, but is very inefficient. The Leibniz formula is often referred to or associated with the symbol: **n!** (n factorial). This alone should inspire caution, as most students of mathematics know, the factorial grows at an alarming rate.

If a matrix consisted entirely of diagonal elements, the determinant is simply the product of these. We already know how to diagonalize a matrix using Gauss-Jordan elimination, which we used to solve the system of equations and to calculate the inverse. A code to accomplish this is listed in Appendix A.

14

Chapter 7. Lagrange Multipliers

Sometimes we want to add constraints to a problem. A common example of this would be a least-squares curve fit that matches exactly at one or more points. This would then be called linear least-squares with linear constraints. Because we cannot achieve the global minimum (in the least-squares sense) and *also* require exact agreement at one or more points, we must somehow *loosen up* the minimization requirement without making the problem nonlinear. This modified goal is accomplished with Lagrange multipliers. In this particular case, we don't care what the value of these terms (the Lagrange multipliers) are, but there are some problems (for example, entropy and free energy) for which these have significance.

The first part of our problem is represented by:

$$[A][X] = [B] \tag{7.1}$$

where **[A]** has dimensions of **mxn**, **[X]** has dimensions **nx1**, and **[B]** has dimensions **mx1**. There will be more data points than adjustable coefficients so that **m>n**, otherwise this would be an exact match and not least-squares. We cannot directly solve a **mxn** system of equations and so we multiply both sides by the transpose of **A**:

$$\left[A^T A\right][X] = \left[A^T B\right] \tag{7.2}$$

This is now an **nxn** set of equations for **n** unknowns, which could be expressed:

$$[X] = \left[A^T A\right]^{-1}\left[A^T B\right] \tag{7.3}$$

The constraints (for example, matching exactly at one or more points) can be represented by this equation:

$$[C][X] = [D] \tag{7.4}$$

The number of columns of **[C]** must match the dimension of **[X]** but may only contain a single row. The number of rows of **[D]** match the number of rows in **[C]**. To implement Lagrange's algorithm, we combine 7.1 and 7.4 to form the augmented matrix:

$$\begin{bmatrix} A & C^T \\ C & 0 \end{bmatrix}\begin{bmatrix} X \\ \Lambda \end{bmatrix} = \begin{bmatrix} B \\ D \end{bmatrix} \tag{7.5}$$

15

Here $[\mathbf{C}^T]$ is the transpose of $[\mathbf{C}]$ and $[\Lambda]$ is the column vector (matrix of dimension **nx1**) containing the Lagrange multipliers. If we expand this augmented matrix and examine each piece we could see that it does indeed satisfy both $\mathbf{AX+C^T\Lambda=B}$ and $\mathbf{CX=D}$. Remember, we can't satisfy both $\mathbf{AX=B}$ and $\mathbf{CX=D}$. In order to add $\mathbf{CX=D}$ as a requirement, we have loosened up $\mathbf{AX=B}$ by adding the term $\mathbf{C^T\Lambda}$. Once we set up 7.5, we simply pass it to the same Gauss-Jordan elimination code to solve it. The *extra* coefficients (i.e., Lagrange multipliers) will be at the end of the list after the values of $[\mathbf{X}]$.

The code for this algorithm (matrix.c) along with several examples can be found in the free associated with this book at the web address listed beneath the Preface.

An Example

Consider the task of fitting a straight line through a series of data points. This is perhaps the most common form of linear least squares. We might simply use the best fit or we might require an exact match at some particular point. Typical data and lines are shown in this next figure:

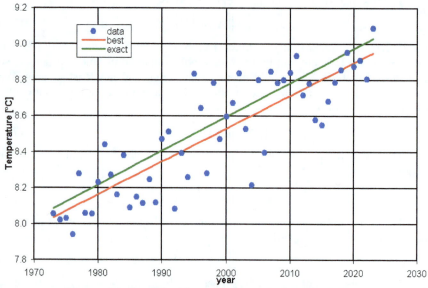

Figure 10. Straight Lines Fit through Scattered Data

The red line above is the best fit, while the green line matches exactly (goes through the data point) at 2000. We can easily solve and graph this problem using Excel™, either with the built-in graphing and trend line features or by using the built-in matrix operations.

We first form the matrix $\mathbf{A}^T\mathbf{A}$ and $\mathbf{A}^T\mathbf{B}$, as shown below:

	$\mathbf{A}^T\mathbf{A}$	$\mathbf{A}^T\mathbf{B}$
51	101,898	433
101,898	203,603,254	865,795

$$(7.6)$$

In this case, the upper left value of $\mathbf{A}^T\mathbf{A}$ is simply the number of data points. The lower left and upper right values are the sum of the years, which we could find using the Excel function =SUM(B2:B52). The lower right value is the sum of the squares of the years, which we could also find using the built-in function =SUMSQ(B2:B52). We can calculate all 2x2 values with s single function call: =MMULT(TRANSPOSE(A2:B52),A2:B52).

The upper value of $\mathbf{A}^T\mathbf{B}$ is the sum of the temperatures, =SUM(C2:C52), and the bottom value is the sum of the product of year times temperature, =SUMPRODUCT(B2:B52,C2:C52). We can calculate 2x1 values with the function call: =MMULT(TRANSPOSE(A2:B52),C2:C52). The matrices are:

	$[\mathbf{A}^T\mathbf{A}]^{-1}$	$[\mathbf{X}]$
361.287	-0.18081448	-27.9884
-0.1808	9.04977E-05	0.01826

$$(7.7)$$

The resulting line is then:

$$y=0.01826*x-27.9884$$

We could simply adjust the constant in the equation above to force the line through the value at 2000 but this wouldn't be the best fit. If we want the best fit (i.e., least square error) while going through the data point at 2000, we must use a Lagrange multiplier. To do so, we form the equation for $\mathbf{C}$ and $\mathbf{D}$, which are:

	$\mathbf{C}$		$\mathbf{D}$
1	2000	8.60

$$(7.8)$$

If we express the linear equation, $y=a+bx$, then the matrix augmenting term above is simply: $a+b*2000=8.60$. We build the augmented matrix (7.5), take the inverse using MINVERSE(), and then multiply the right-hand side to obtain:

355.429	-0.17771459	-17.1269	-29.111
-0.1777	8.88573E-05	0.009063	0.018854
-17.127	0.009063444	-50.0755	-3.28246

$$(7.9)$$

The best-fit constrained line is then:

$$y=0.018854*x-29.111$$

which is not the same as we would have gotten by simply adjusting the constant, **a**, or moving the same line up or down to go through the desired point. At this point we could easily calculate the difference in the residual between the two approximations. The error for the best unconstrained fit is 1.393, for the adjusted unconstrained fit is 1.602, and for the constrained best fit is 1.598. Not surprisingly, the unconstrained does fit better than the constrained, which will always be the case for this sort of problem. The data, calculations, and graph may be found in the spreadsheet temperature.xls in the free online archive at the web address listed beneath the Preface.

Chapter 8. Vandermomde

Fitting a curve through a collection of points, such as the straight line example in the previous chapter is a common problem. The concept and implementation is simple. As we increase the order of the curve-fit, however, the task may become more difficult. We may, for example, want to consider an equation like:

$$y = a + bx + cx^2 + dx^3 + ... \qquad (8.1)$$

Excel™ will add a trend line to of order up to 6 and provide the coefficients automatically. In this case the matrix **[A]** will be:

$$A = \begin{bmatrix} 1 & X_1 & X_1^2 & X_1^3 \\ 1 & X_2 & X_2^2 & X_2^3 \\ 1 & X_3 & X_3^2 & X_3^3 \\ 1 & X_n & X_n^2 & X_n^3 \end{bmatrix} \qquad (8.2)$$

This matrix is called a Vandermonde.[5] With many points this matrix can get quite large. When we form the least-squares basis matrix, $A^T A$, the values can get *very* large. When we try to solve this by reducing it to upper triangular form using Gauss-Jordan elimination, our results may be overwhelmed by round-off error because we are adding and subtracting very large numbers, which are fairly close to each other, especially if the data points are clustered.

Precision Options

Before the ubiquitous availability of Intel™ FPUs, such computations were often carried out using single-precision (32-bit) floating-point arithmetic (i.e., floats). Full row and column pivoting (as described in Chapter 4) rescued many—but not all—such calculations. Thankfully, double-precision (64-bit) floating-point arithmetic (i.e., doubles) is standard on all modern machines. Still, sometimes with extremely large problems, even this is not sufficient. An example of such a problem is illustrated in Figure 1 (page i), which is a global barometric pressure regression involving many thousands of data points sprinkled around the world. Without jumping to quadruple-precision (128-bit)

---

[5] Named after the French mathematician, Alexandre-Théophile Vandermonde.

19

and beyond operations, which is possible on Intel machines using software (see discussion and free software described elsewhere[6]), there is another option...

Intel FPUs actually perform all calculations using 80-bit numbers (floating-point and integers, both of which can be quite handy). If you are very careful how you prepare the C code, you can do everything with 80-bit precision on an Intel machine. However—and this is the problem—if any step isn't 80-bit, the precision will be lost converting between 80-bit and 64-bit values. The Microsoft™ 16-bit C compiler (Version 7.0, which I still have a copy of for this very reason) will compile such code using "long double" designation for 80-bit. The sad thing is that this capability ended with the Microsoft 32-bit compiler and Visual Studio™ so that this capability is no longer available—in software. The hardware still works. Of course, you can still accomplish this by writing code in assembler, as discussed elsewhere.[7] You can verify the ability or lack thereof in a compiler with the following statement:

```
printf("%i bytes\n",sizeof(long double));
```

which will be 10 bytes for 80-bit and 8 bytes for 64-bits. If you don't have MSCV700 and 32-bit Windows O/S, you can use the 128-bit (or whatever; it's adjustable) free software.

---

[6] Benton, D. James, *Numerical Calculus: Differentiation and Integration*, ISBN-9781980680901, Amazon, 2018.
[7] Benton, D. James, *CPUnleashed! Tapping Processor Speed*, ISBN-9798421420361, Amazon, 2022.

Chapter 8. Simple Iterative Solutions

Many large matrix problems arise from solving partial differential equations rather than curve-fitting data. Perhaps the most common partial differential equation solved across many fields from conduction to diffusion to inviscid flow is Laplace's:

$$\frac{\partial^2 T}{\partial x^2} + \frac{\partial^2 T}{\partial y^2} + \frac{\partial^2 T}{\partial z^2} = 0 \tag{8.1}$$

The finite difference form of the second partial differential is often expressed:

$$\frac{\partial^2 T}{\partial x^2} = \frac{T_{t,x+\Delta x} - 2T_{t,x} + T_{t,x-\Delta x}}{\Delta x^2} \tag{8.2}$$

We can construct an array containing the equations for all of the nodes. There will be boundary conditions so that some of the equations will be different, for example, an isothermal boundary: $T_{47}=1000$ or an insulated boundary: $\partial T/\partial x)_{56}=0$ or a convection boundary: $\partial T/\partial x)_{83}=h*(T_{83}-T_0)$. The assembled matrix may look something like this:

1	-1	0	0	0	0
-1	**2**	-1	0	0	0
0	-1	**2**	-1	0	0
0	0	-1	**2**	-1	0
0	0	0	-1	**2**	-1
0	0	0	0	-1	**1**

$$(8.3)$$

The diagonal elements are shown in bold. In this case the diagonal coefficients are as large or larger (absolute value) than the off-diagonal ones. If this is the case, we can begin with a guess and easily calculate new estimates of each unknown by moving all off-diagonal terms to the right side and dividing by the diagonal:

$$x_2 = \frac{b_2 + x_1 + x_3}{2} \tag{8.4}$$

21

This approach is called the Gauss-Seidel or Liebmann method[8], is simple to implement and works fairly well. If the matrix is diagonally dominant, this method will eventually converge. If it isn't diagonally dominant and it doesn't converge, we might try to dampen the iterations:

$$x_{2,new} = \frac{x_{2,old} + \left(\dfrac{b_2 + x_1 + x_3}{2}\right)}{2} \tag{8.5}$$

but this rarely works, so don't count on it. This idea does, however, inspire a modified approach in which we step a little farther, rather than less. This is called the Successive Over-Relaxation (SOR) method. The iterations are:

$$x_{2,new} = (1 - \omega)x_{2,old} + \omega\left(\frac{b_2 + x_1 + x_3}{2}\right) \tag{8.6}$$

where the relaxation parameter, ω, is greater than one ($\omega > 1$). If ω were less than one ($\omega < 1$), this would be Successive *Under*-Relaxation. Many articles have been published on the magic value of ω that will yield the fastest results. These are perhaps interesting but of no practical value, as each problem is different and there is no reason why the magic value of ω that works best for one problem will provide optimal results for yours. Typical values for ω are between 4/3 (1.333) and 3/2 (1.5).

<u>An Example</u>

As an example of these algorithms (G-S and SOR), we consider steady-state conduction (or diffusion) in a 2D plane with simple boundary conditions, such as illustrated below:

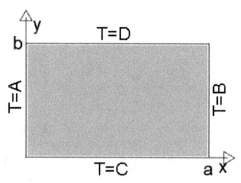

Figure 11. Conduction Example Domain

[8] Liebmann, H., "Die Angenaherte Ermittlung Harmonischer Funktionen und Konformer Abbildungen (The Approximate Determination of Harmonic Functions and Conformal Maps)," Sitzungsber, Münchener, Vol. 47, pp. 385-416, 1918

The calculations and code can be found in tband.c within the free archive at the web address listed beneath the Preface. A snippet of the G-S code appears below:

```
for(iter=0;iter<nx*ny;iter++)
  {
  for(i=1;i<ny-1;i++)
    {
    for(j=1;j<nx-1;j++)
      {
      k=nx*i+j;
      xk=x[k];
      x[k]=(b[k]-a1[k]*x[k-nx]-a2[k]*x[k+nx]
        -a4[k]*x[k+1]-a5[k]*x[k-1])/a3[k];
      }
    }
  }
```

Here is a snippet of the SOR code showing the slight differences:

```
for(iter=0;iter<nx*ny;iter++)
  {
  for(i=1;i<ny-1;i++)
    {
    for(j=1;j<nx-1;j++)
      {
      k=nx*i+j;
      xk=x[k];
      x[k]=(b[k]-a1[k]*x[k-nx]-a2[k]*x[k+nx]
        -a4[k]*x[k+1]-a5[k]*x[k-1])/a3[k];
      x[k]=omega*x[k]+(1.-omega)*xk;
      }
    }
  }
```

The grid for this example is 400x400 or 160,000 nodes. Even at this size, it takes only a few seconds to solve the equations. The output of the code is listed below:

```
TBAND/V3.0: Test Banded matrix solvers
by Dudley J. Benton
solving the Laplace Equation with
Dirichlet boundary conditions
number of grid points=400*400=160000
creating banded matrix
solving using Gauss-Seidel
error=0, reduction=1.99992E-005
solving using Successive Over Relaxation
error=0, reduction=1.99989E-005
saving solution: tband.tb2
```

The results are written out to a file (tband.tb2) and are shown in this next figure:

23

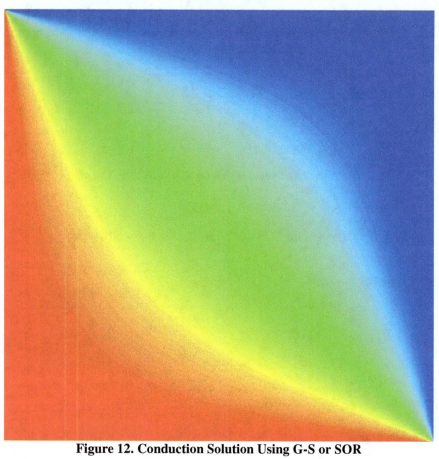
Figure 12. Conduction Solution Using G-S or SOR

Chapter 9. Conjugate-Gradient Method

Laplace's Equation is often easy to solve; however, there are more difficult ones. Just by adding a right-hand side, we obtain Poisson's Equation, which can be quite a challenge at times:

$$\nabla^2 \psi = \frac{\partial^2 \psi}{\partial x^2} + \frac{\partial^2 \psi}{\partial y^2} + \frac{\partial^2 \psi}{\partial z^2} = -\omega \qquad (9.1)$$

One application that I have solved many times and in many ways is open channel flow. The computer model I found most useful for this purpose is EFDC (Environmental Fluid Dynamics Code) developed by John Hamrick. I optimized the FORTRAN code and added dynamic array allocation in 1996 while working on a joint project. I also implemented an improved solution technique, as the governing partial differential equation is more *stiff* than Laplace's equation and can require many iterations using G-S or SOR. See Appendix D for details.

Another iterative method, which is similar to but may be considerably faster than G-S and SOR called the Conjugate-Gradient or Hestenes-Stiefel method[9]. Gauss-Seidel is basically a successive substitution, separating the off-diagonal elements from the diagonal ones; whereas, the Conjugate-Gradient method is a repeated vector projection with each successive vector approximation to the solution mutually perpendicular to the preceding ones so that theoretically, the final solution must be found in **n** steps, where **n** is the rank of the matrix. In practice, an adequate approximation to the solution is often found in far fewer than **n** steps, making this an attractive approach. The algorithm is somewhat more complicated, but the extra effort can be well worth it in computational savings and there is another benefit that we will discuss later in this chapter.

The C-G approach is best understood in terms of vectors. The basic problem **[A][X]=[B]** can be rearranged to produce a residual: **[B]-[A][X]=[R]**, where **[R]** is the residual obtained with each estimate of the solution, **[X]**. The sum of the squares of the residual is $\mathbf{R^2=[R^T][R]}$, where $\mathbf{[R^T]}$ is the transpose of **[R]**. We define a step size along the direction between the previous and current estimates of the solution such that the $\mathbf{R^2}$ is minimized. We then take another step that is orthogonal (perpendicular) the previous step and repeat the process (recall the

---

[9] Hestenes, M. R. and E. Stiefel, "Methods of Conjugate Gradients for Solving Linear Systems," *Journal of Research National Bureau of Standards*, Vol. 49, No. 6, pp. 409–436, 1952.

perpendicular vectors in Chapter 2). The C-G method is truly remarkable in it's efficiency. Here's a simple function to implement it:

```
double D[n],Q[n],R[n];
void ConjugateGradient(double*A,double*B,double*X,
    int*J,int n,int m)
  {
  int i,iter,k,l;
  double a,b,dTq,q,r,rTr;
  for(i=0;i<n;i++)
    X[i]=0.;
  for(rTr=l=i=0;i<n;i++)
    {
    r=B[i];
    for(k=0;k<m;k++,l++)
      if(J[l]>=0)
        r-=A[l]*X[J[l]];
    D[i]=R[i]=r;
    rTr+=r*r;
    }
  for(iter=0;;iter++)
    {
    for(dTq=l=i=0;i<n;i++)
      {
      for(q=k=0;k<m;k++,l++)
        if(J[l]>=0)
          q+=A[l]*D[J[l]];
      Q[i]=q;
      dTq+=D[i]*q;
      }
    a=rTr/dTq;
    for(i=0;i<n;i++)
      X[i]+=a*D[i];
    b=rTr;
    for(rTr=i=0;i<n;i++)
      {
      R[i]-=a*Q[i];
      rTr+=R[i]*R[i];
      }
    b=rTr/b;
    for(i=0;i<n;i++)
      D[i]=R[i]-b*D[i];
    if(rTr<FLT_EPSILON)
      break;
    }
  }
```

This code along with sample inputs can be found in the on-line archive in file cg.c. This code also contains a function for the Gauss-Siedel method for comparison. Typical output for both methods is:

```
begin Gauss-Siedel
iter=0, rTr=2.16423
iter=1, rTr=0.666334
iter=2, rTr=0.253819
iter=3, rTr=0.10727
iter=4, rTr=0.0472994
iter=5, rTr=0.0211947
iter=6, rTr=0.00953969
iter=7, rTr=0.00429109
iter=8, rTr=0.00192536
iter=9, rTr=0.000861461
iter=10, rTr=0.000384466
iter=11, rTr=0.000171226
iter=12, rTr=7.6131E-005
iter=13, rTr=3.38061E-005
iter=14, rTr=1.49969E-005
iter=15, rTr=6.64784E-006
iter=16, rTr=2.9452E-006
iter=17, rTr=1.30426E-006
iter=18, rTr=5.77393E-007
iter=19, rTr=2.55549E-007
iter=20, rTr=1.13083E-007
begin Conjugate-Gradient
iter=0, rTr=4.50617
iter=1, rTr=0.00476629
iter=2, rTr=0.000302086
iter=3, rTr=1.40871E-005
iter=4, rTr=9.45145E-006
iter=5, rTr=2.41304E-006
iter=6, rTr=3.11957E-007
iter=7, rTr=1.58797E-007
...
9 1 1.00005
10 0.897275 0.897297
11 0.825709 0.825673
12 0.78056 0.780504
13 0.747423 0.747343
14 0.709131 0.709081
15 0.638209 0.638171
16 0.468704 0.468711
17 0 0
18 1 1.00005
19 0.763393 0.763394
20 0.625 0.624949
21 0.549107 0.549008
22 0.5 0.499922
23 0.450893 0.450809
24 0.375 0.374952
...
```

I chose marginally ill-conditioned **[A]** and initial estimate **[X]**={0} for the C-G method just to illustrate the point that this method will converge eventually, regardless of the initial estimate. The underlying problem is a transient response to periodic stimuli. The solution is shown in this next figure:

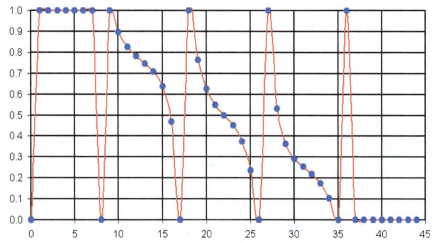

Figure 13. Solution Using Conjugate-Gradient Method

Chapter 10. Singular Value Decomposition of a Matrix

There are many ways of analyzing matrices. One of the most interesting is the singular value decomposition. Any matrix can be represented as a product of three matrices, each with special characteristics. These are the left and right eigenvectors ([U] and [V]) and the singular values ([S]). The form is:

$$[A] = [U]^T [S][V] \qquad (10.1)$$

The eigenvectors are orthonormal, that is, they are both orthogonal and have a magnitude of unity (i.e., sum of the squares equals one). The orthonormal conditions means that:

$$[U]^T [U] = [V]^T [V] = [I] \qquad (10.2)$$

where [I] is the identify matrix (i.e., ones on the diagonal and zeroes elsewhere). If [A] is symmetric, the left and right eigenvectors are complementary, [V]=[U]^T. (i.e., [V] is the transpose of [U]). The matrix [S] is diagonal (i.e. like the identity matrix, non-zero on the diagonal and zeroes elsewhere). If [A] is also positive definite, all of the eigenvalues are greater than zero. If [A] is singular (i.e., degenerate), one or more of the eigenvalues are zero. The number of rows and columns in [A] need not be equal.

If we were considering nodes along a vibrating beam, the matrix relating the stiffness and displacement could be expressed in terms of a singular value decomposition. The eigenvectors would be the modal shapes, which are sin(x), sin(2x), sin(3x), and/or cos(x), cos(2x), cos(3x), etc., depending on the end conditions. The singular values would be the square of the resonant frequencies. This is how orthogonal functions enter the discussion: eigenvectors are the orthogonal functions and eigenvalues are the coefficients. Any matrix—including an image—can be represented by a singular value decomposition. The question becomes, "Is there something to be gained here?" The answer is, "Yes!"

Since the eigenvectors are orthonormal, the contribution from any trio (left eigenvector, right eigenvector, singular value) is no larger than the magnitude of the singular value. If we arrange the eigenvectors and singular values such that the largest one is at the top left and the smallest at the bottom right, we can readily see the relative importance (i.e., contribution to the whole) of each part. For many images, the size of the singular values falls off quickly so that most of the information is contained in the first few, while the rest are just noise. If we're transmitting an image back from Pluto, we don't have to send the whole thing, just the most significant content and we have a way of answering the age-old question, "How much is enough?"

Perhaps the earliest method for decomposing a matrix in this way was developed by von Mises and is called the *Power Method*.[10] This approach follows the line of reasoning that if you multiply a vector over and over again, normalizing each time, eventually the largest (or most significant) term will dominate. This is coupled with deflation so that the matrix (hopefully) eventually reduces to the desired form. This method may work for some small matrices but is not robust and is inefficient, especially when there are better methods available. The code to accomplish this (svd.c, function P0werMeth0d) may be found in the archive.

A better approach is called Givens Rotations.[11] The idea here is to eliminate one term in the matrix with each step. This method does work but is quite slow and can stumble over large problems. The code to accomplish this (givens.c) may also be found in the archive. The most effective and efficient method is called Householder Transformations.[12] You will find the code in archive in file svd.c, which also includes test cases and comparisons between the methods. For illustration, we will consider the following simple matrix:

$$[A]=\begin{array}{|c|c|c|c|}\hline 1 & 1 & 1 & 1 \\\hline 1 & 2 & 4 & 8 \\\hline 1 & 3 & 9 & 27 \\\hline 1 & 4 & 16 & 64 \\\hline\end{array}\qquad(10.3)$$

You may recognize this as the left hand side of $y=a+bx+cx^2+dx^3$, $x=1, 2, 3, 4$, which is a Vandermonde. The singular value decomposition is in three parts: the left eigenvectors:

$$[U]=\begin{array}{|c|c|c|c|}\hline -0.0199 & -0.0701 & -0.2567 & -0.9637 \\\hline 0.3438 & 0.5523 & 0.7208 & -0.2393 \\\hline -0.7880 & -0.2667 & 0.5440 & -0.1092 \\\hline 0.5103 & -0.7867 & 0.3444 & -0.0451 \\\hline\end{array}\qquad(10.4)$$

---

[10] von Mises, R. and H. Pollaczek-Geiringer, "Praktische Verfahren der Gleichungsauflösung," *ZAMM - Zeitschrift für Angewandte Mathematik und Mechanik* Vol. 9, pp. 152-164, 1929.

[11] Named after Wallace Givens, who developed this technique in the early 1950s while working at Argonne National Laboratory.

[12] Householder, A. S., "Unitary Triangularization of a Nonsymmetric Matrix" *Journal of the ACM*, Vol. 5, No. 4, pp. 339–342, 1958

the singular values:

$$[S]=\begin{array}{|c|c|c|c|}
\hline
72.55 & 0 & 0 & 0 \\
\hline
0 & 3.655 & 0 & 0 \\
\hline
0 & 0 & 0.7303 & 0 \\
\hline
0 & 0 & 0 & 0.06196 \\
\hline
\end{array}$$

(10.5)

the right eigenvectors:

$$[V]=\begin{array}{|c|c|c|c|}
\hline
-0.0181 & -0.1226 & -0.3937 & -0.9109 \\
\hline
0.3769 & 0.6613 & 0.5546 & -0.3362 \\
\hline
-0.8489 & -0.0262 & 0.4917 & -0.1921 \\
\hline
0.3702 & -0.7395 & 0.5438 & -0.1428 \\
\hline
\end{array}$$

(10.6)

The equivalent matrix **[A]** can easily be generated for any order. The program svd.c performs this as a loop that you can adjust. The eigenvectors can be sequentially orthogonalized using the modified Gram-Schmidt[13] procedure, but this can be problematic. The orthogonalization procedure is handled by:

```
for(i=0;i<k;i++)
  {
  p=dotproduct(v+cols*k,v+cols*i,cols);
  for(j=0;j<cols;j++)
    v[cols*k+j]-=p*v[cols*i+j];
  normalize(v+cols*k,cols);
  }
```

The dot product and normalization functions are simple:

```
double dotproduct(double*u,double*v,int n)
  {
  int i;
  double p;
  for(p=i=0;i<n;i++)
    p+=u[i]*v[i];
  return(p);
  }
void normalize(double*v,int n)
  {
  int i;
  double vv;
  vv=l2norm(v,n);
```

---

[13] Pursell, L. and S. Y. Trimble, "Gram-Schmidt Orthogonalization by Gauss Elimination", *The American Mathematical Monthly*, Vol. 98, No. 6, pp. 544–549, 1991.

```
for(i=0;i<n;i++)
  v[i]/=vv;
}
```

The left eigenvalues can be estimated from the right ones and then orthogonalized in the same way.

```
multiply(a,v+cols*k,u+rows*k,rows,cols,1);
normalize(u+rows*k,rows);
for(i=0;i<k;i++)
  {
  p=dotproduct(u+rows*k,u+rows*i,rows);
  for(j=0;j<rows;j++)
    u[rows*k+j]-=p*u[rows*i+j];
  normalize(u+rows*k,rows);
  }
```

All of these patches are included in svd.c, which yields the following for the Power Method applied to the same problem as before:

```
using Power Method
[u]=0.137729 0.807899 0.573
    0.430706 0.472101 -0.769164
    0.891921 -0.352731 0.282945
[s]=10.6031 1.24544 0.151452
[v]=0.137729 0.430706 0.891921
    0.807899 0.472101 -0.352731
    0.573 -0.769164 0.282945
[uT][u]=1 0 0
        0 1 0
        0 0 1
[vT][v]=1 0 0
        0 1 0
        0 0 1
[uT][s][v]=0.711908 0.778327 1.15153
           1.62423 4.00821 7.4179
           0.0874157 2.13158 5.76896
```

Note the discrepancy in eigenvalues: 10.6031 (10.6496), 1.24544 (1.2507), 0.151452 (0.150156). Also the discrepancy in the last row of the reconstructed matrix: 0.0874157 (was 1), 2.13158 (was 3), 5.76896 (was 9). If it's this bad for a 3x3 matrix, you can imagine the error for a 4096x4096 or larger one.

One very interesting application of the singular value decomposition is image reduction. The eigenvectors have unit magnitude; therefore, the contribution of each eigenvector is directly proportional to the eigenvalue. If you decompose an image in this way, you know how much information you're leaving out by discarding terms. This approach has been used to pack and transmit images from space.

32

Chapter 11. Potential to Gradient

The problem illustrated in Figure 1 of the global barometric pressure field is a solution to Laplace's Equation (8.1) over a domain consisting of triangles:

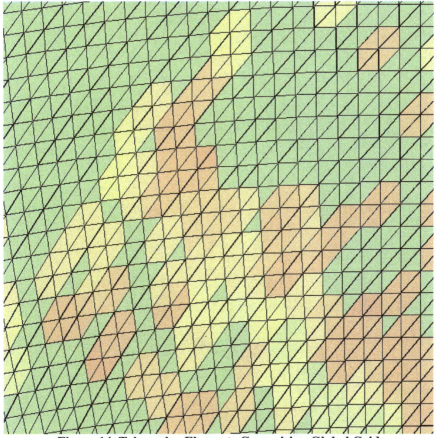

Figure 14. Triangular Elements Comprising Global Grid

Solution is simple: 1) assign values to each node closest to a meteorological station reporting data; 2) calculate values at all of the other points by averaging the surrounding points; 3) repeat until the differences are insignificant. Each triangular element can be represented:

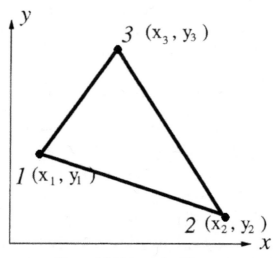

Figure 15. Triangular Element

A linear function (for example pressure, **p**) varying over this element could be represented:

$$p = a + bx + cy \qquad (11.1)$$

We can find **a**, **b**, and **c** as in Chapter 4 using matrices:

$$\begin{bmatrix} 1 & x_1 & y_1 \\ 1 & x_2 & y_2 \\ 1 & x_3 & y_3 \end{bmatrix} \begin{bmatrix} a \\ b \\ c \end{bmatrix} = \begin{bmatrix} p_1 \\ p_2 \\ p_3 \end{bmatrix} \qquad (11.2)$$

The gradient of the pressure is a vector defined by:

$$\frac{\partial p}{\partial x}\hat{i} + \frac{\partial p}{\partial y}\hat{j} = b\hat{i} + c\hat{j} \qquad (11.3)$$

The constants for this element (**a**, **b**, and **c**) are found by inverting the first matrix:

$$\begin{bmatrix} a \\ b \\ c \end{bmatrix} = \begin{bmatrix} 1 & x_1 & y_1 \\ 1 & x_2 & y_2 \\ 1 & x_3 & y_3 \end{bmatrix}^{-1} \begin{bmatrix} p_1 \\ p_2 \\ p_3 \end{bmatrix} \qquad (11.4)$$

The inverse of the matrix can be found analytically to be:

$$\begin{bmatrix} \dfrac{x_2 y_3 - y_2 x_3}{\det} & \dfrac{y_1 x_3 - x_1 y_3}{\det} & \dfrac{x_1 y_2 - y_1 x_2}{\det} \\[2mm] \dfrac{y_2 - y_3}{\det} & \dfrac{y_3 - y_1}{\det} & \dfrac{y_1 - y_2}{\det} \\[2mm] \dfrac{x_3 - x_2}{\det} & \dfrac{x_1 - x_3}{\det} & \dfrac{x_2 - x_1}{\det} \end{bmatrix} \qquad (11.5)$$

$$\det = x_2 y_3 - y_2 x_3 - x_1 y_3 + y_1 x_3 + x_1 y_2 - y_1 x_2$$

Wind is driven by differences in barometric pressure. The wind speed and direction is proportional to and in line with the negative of the gradient of the barometric pressure. We can, therefore, calculate the direction and scale at the center of each triangular element by applying the equation above to the three pressures at the corners. The pressure contours are:

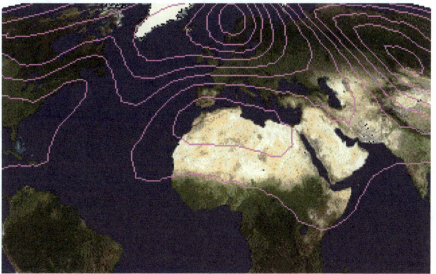

Figure 16. Barometric Pressure Contours

35

The resulting wind vectors are:

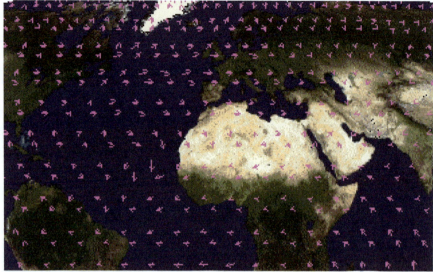

Figure 17. Wind Vectors

Both of these operations are included in the versatile plotting program, TP2, which is available free at the website listed below the Preface. For example:

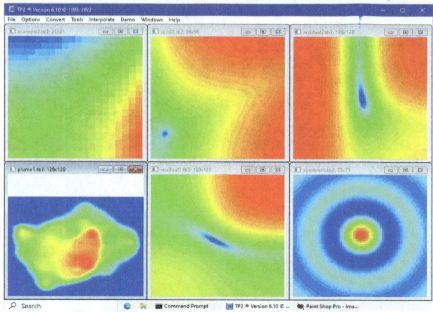

Figure 18. Typical 2D Fields (Topological Surfaces)

These 2D fields can be converted to 2D vectors using the array above:

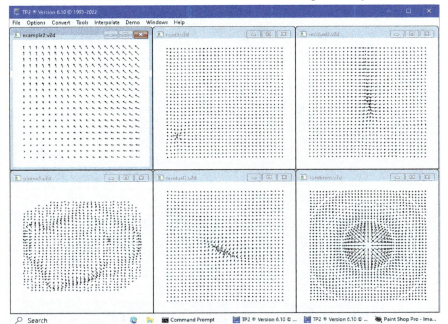

Figure 19. Previous Fields into Gradient Vectors

TP2 also has several options for converting scattered 2D or 3D data into smooth field. The data might look something like the following:

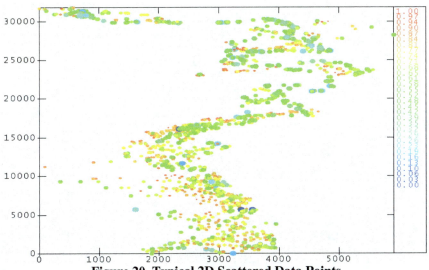

Figure 20. Typical 2D Scattered Data Points

The equivalent 3D linear basis function for a tetrahedron is:

$$p = a + bx + cy + dz \qquad (11.6)$$

The equivalent 4x4 3D matrix is:

$$\begin{bmatrix} 1 & x_1 & y_1 & z_1 \\ 1 & x_2 & y_2 & z_2 \\ 1 & x_3 & y_3 & z_3 \\ 1 & x_4 & y_4 & z_4 \end{bmatrix} \begin{bmatrix} a \\ b \\ c \\ d \end{bmatrix} = \begin{bmatrix} p_1 \\ p_2 \\ p_3 \\ p_4 \end{bmatrix} \qquad (11.7)$$

The inverse is much too complex to list in symbolic form but here is the code:

```
d=(-x2*y3*z4+x2*z3*y4+x3*y2*z4-x3*z2*y4-x4*y2*z3
   +x4*z2*y3+x1*y3*z4-x1*z3*y4-x3*y1*z4+
x3*z1*y4+x4*y1*z3-x4*z1*y3-x1*y2*z4+x1*z2*y4+x2*y1*z4
   -x2*z1*y4-x4*y1*z2+x4*z1*
y2+x1*y2*z3-x1*z2*y3-x2*y1*z3+x2*z1*y3+x3*y1*z2
   -x3*z1*y2)
A[0][0]=-(x2*y3*z4-x2*z3*y4-x3*y2*z4+x3*z2*y4+x4*y2*z3
   -x4*z2*y3)/d;
A[0][1]= (x1*y3*z4-x1*z3*y4-x3*y1*z4+x3*z1*y4+x4*y1*z3
   -x4*z1*y3)/d;
A[0][2]=-(x1*y2*z4-x1*z2*y4-x2*y1*z4+x2*z1*y4+x4*y1*z2
   -x4*z1*y2)/d;
A[0][3]= (x1*y2*z3-x1*z2*y3-x2*y1*z3+x2*z1*y3+x3*y1*z2
   -x3*z1*y2)/d;
A[1][0]= (y3*z4-z3*y4-y2*z4+z2*y4+y2*z3-z2*y3)/d;
A[1][1]=-(y3*z4-z3*y4-y1*z4+z1*y4+y1*z3-z1*y3)/d;
A[1][2]= (y2*z4-z2*y4-y1*z4+z1*y4+y1*z2-z1*y2)/d;
A[1][3]=-(y2*z3-z2*y3-y1*z3+z1*y3+y1*z2-z1*y2)/d;
A[2][0]=-(x3*z4-z3*x4-x2*z4+z2*x4+x2*z3-z2*x3)/d;
A[2][1]= (x3*z4-z3*x4-x1*z4+z1*x4+x1*z3-z1*x3)/d;
A[2][2]=-(x2*z4-z2*x4-x1*z4+z1*x4+x1*z2-z1*x2)/d;
A[2][3]= (x2*z3-z2*x3-x1*z3+z1*x3+x1*z2-z1*x2)/d;
A[3][0]= (x3*y4-y3*x4-x2*y4+y2*x4+x2*y3-y2*x3)/d;
A[3][1]=-(x3*y4-y3*x4-x1*y4+y1*x4+x1*y3-y1*x3)/d;
A[3][2]= (x2*y4-y2*x4-x1*y4+y1*x4+x1*y2-y1*x2)/d;
A[3][3]=-(x2*y3-y2*x3-x1*y3+y1*x3+x1*y2-y1*x2)/d;
```

A typical 3D field is shown here like a block as seen from the top and two sides:

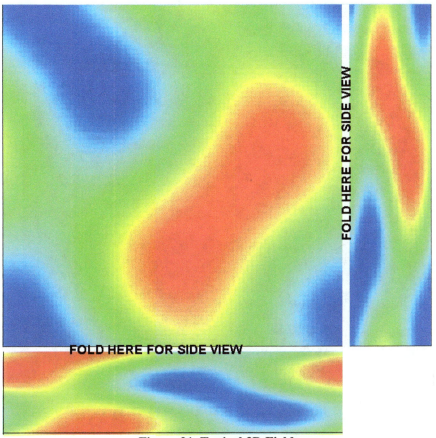

Figure 21. Typical 3D Field

This information is easily converted to gradients and represented as 3D vectors:

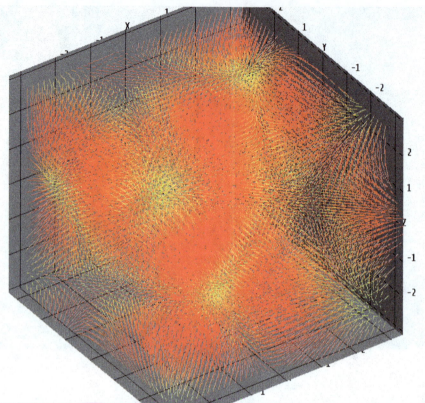

Figure 22. Typical 3D Gradient Vectors

Chapter 12. Vectorizable Methods

The concept of vectorization has already been introduced. We will now consider this in more detail. The question is: can a method be implemented using a series of loops by performing operations on values that are physically located in contiguous memory? If not, the method is not vectorizable. If a method is vectorizable, we may be able to increase the speed by using specialized code and/or hardware to perform the repetitive tasks. For example, the Gauss-Seidel and Successive Over-Relaxation methods are not vectorizable; whereas, the Jacobi and Conjugate Gradient methods are.

The Jacobi method is slower than the Gauss-Seidel so we might want to consider it here; however, the Jacobi method can fail depending on the arrangement of the matrix, especially if it isn't diagonally dominant. This option is not attractive. Gauss-Seidel is robust, fast, and simple to implement. Conjugate Gradient is robust, fast, and more difficult to implement, but it is vectorizable and from that we can gain some advantage. See, for example, Appendix D.

$$\begin{bmatrix} a_{00} & a_{01} & a_{02} & 0 & 0 & 0 & 0 & 0 \\ a_{10} & a_{11} & a_{12} & a_{13} & 0 & 0 & 0 & 0 \\ a_{20} & a_{21} & a_{22} & a_{23} & a_{24} & 0 & 0 & 0 \\ 0 & a_{31} & a_{32} & a_{33} & a_{34} & a_{35} & 0 & 0 \\ 0 & 0 & a_{42} & a_{43} & a_{44} & a_{45} & a_{46} & 0 \\ 0 & 0 & 0 & a_{53} & a_{54} & a_{55} & a_{56} & a_{57} \\ 0 & 0 & 0 & 0 & a_{64} & a_{65} & a_{66} & a_{67} \\ 0 & 0 & 0 & 0 & 0 & a_{75} & a_{76} & a_{77} \end{bmatrix}$$

Figure 23. Banded Matrix

Most extremely large matrix problems are of the banded or sparse variety; that is, there are significant portions of the matrix filled with zeroes. While we might solve these using a vectorizable algorithm, the speed advantage will not likely make up for performing many more pointless operations. We could, however, when using vector instructions coded in assembler skip over the zero elements. While this might sound good, it probably won't work to our advantage if performed on an Intel™ processor, as these have a pre-processor that will *stumble* over the skipped operations, resulting in a *jittering* effect that may be even slower overall.

$$
\begin{bmatrix}
1.0 & 0.3 & 0.2 & 1.5 & 0.2 & 0.3 & 0.0 & 0.0 & 0.0 \\
0.1 & 0.5 & 1.3 & 2.5 & 0.8 & 0.4 & 0.0 & 0.0 & 0.0 \\
9.2 & 1.3 & 4.5 & 7.2 & 0.8 & 0.2 & 0.0 & 0.0 & 0.0 \\
0.0 & 0.0 & 0.0 & 0.2 & 1.6 & 0.5 & 0.0 & 0.0 & 0.0 \\
0.0 & 0.0 & 0.0 & 0.4 & 1.8 & 4.2 & 0.0 & 0.0 & 0.0 \\
0.0 & 0.0 & 0.0 & 1.8 & 0.6 & 3.3 & 0.0 & 0.0 & 0.0 \\
0.2 & 1.8 & 0.8 & 0.0 & 0.0 & 0.0 & 0.2 & 0.4 & 1.8 \\
0.7 & 1.6 & 0.7 & 0.0 & 0.0 & 0.0 & 0.8 & 0.6 & 1.2 \\
0.9 & 1.7 & 0.9 & 0.0 & 0.0 & 0.0 & 1.2 & 0.8 & 0.9
\end{bmatrix}
$$

Figure 24. Sparse Matrix

Banded matrices, such as the one shown above, often have patterns and rarely have gaps that we might call *random*. For this reason it is preferable to tailor one of the more robust algorithms to best fit with the patterns for a particular application.

Chapter 13. Animations, 3D Rendering, and Color Depth

One of the more common tasks involving linear algebra is 3D rendering. Points in 3D space are conveniently represented as matrixes, such as:

$$\begin{bmatrix} x \\ y \\ z \end{bmatrix}$$ (13.1)

Rotations can be performed by matrix multiplication. A rotation about the x-axis by an angle θ is performed by the following matrix operation:

$$\begin{bmatrix} 1 & 0 & 0 \\ 0 & \cos(\theta) & -\sin(\theta) \\ 0 & \sin(\theta) & \cos(\theta) \end{bmatrix}$$ (13.2)

A rotation about the y-axis by an angle φ is performed by the following matrix operation:

$$\begin{bmatrix} \cos(\phi) & 0 & \sin(\phi) \\ 0 & 1 & 0 \\ -\sin(\phi) & 0 & \cos(\phi) \end{bmatrix}$$ (13.3)

A rotation about the z-axis by an angle ψ is performed by the following matrix operation:

$$\begin{bmatrix} \cos(\psi) & -\sin(\psi) & 0 \\ \sin(\psi\theta) & \cos(\psi) & 0 \\ 0 & 0 & 1 \end{bmatrix}$$ (13.4)

OpenGL™ performs these operations for you, but it is important to understand what it's doing, plus you may have reason to manually implement them. One reason for doing this may not be readily apparent. Since the beginning of the Web, the standard for animated images has been the GIF (Graphics Interchange Format). More recently, the AVI (Audio-Visual Interleave) and various forms of the Moving Picture Experts Group (MPEG) format are now common. These latter formats can be problematic, as various

43

compression algorithms are used, which are patented and require one or more CODECs (coder-decoder or compression-decompression) add-on modules, some of which demand payment for use. While many of these are readily available in the US, some are only available through payment in other parts of the world or entirely unavailable in areas subject to various international sanctions. Invest a lot of time and effort creating an animation using one of these latter formats and at least part of your intended audience may not be able to view them. This has never been a problem with GIFs, which may often be much smaller than the other formats.

There are two big differences between a GIF and AVI or MPG: 1) limited colors and 2) lossless compression. GIFs are limited to 256 colors, while AVI and MPG are not. No information (details) are lost when creating a GIF; however, the AVI and MPG compression algorithms are *lossy* (information is permanently lost in the process). Consider the following example:

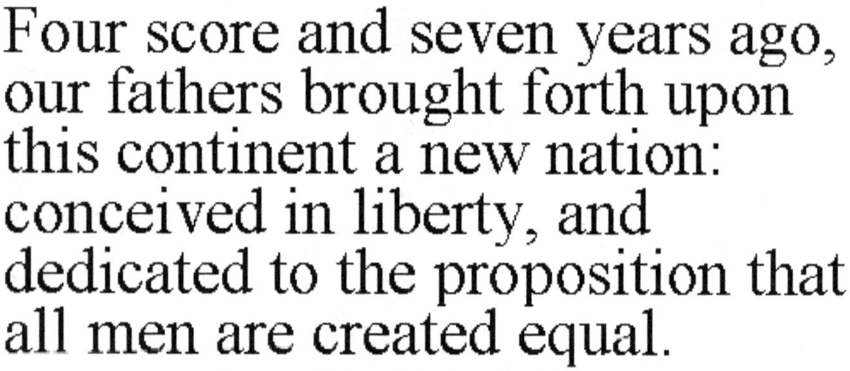

Four score and seven years ago, our fathers brought forth upon this continent a new nation: conceived in liberty, and dedicated to the proposition that all men are created equal.

Figure 25. Text Saved in GIF Format

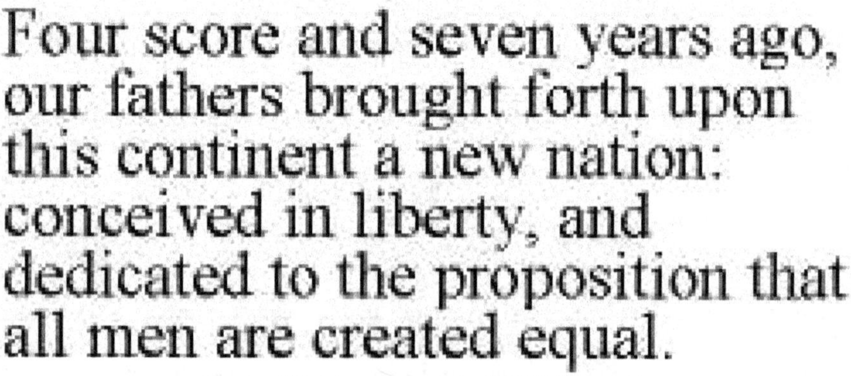

Four score and seven years ago, our fathers brought forth upon this continent a new nation: conceived in liberty, and dedicated to the proposition that all men are created equal.

Figure 26. Text Saved in JPEG Format

This is what *lossy* compression means. Look closer at this zoomed portion:

Four score
our fathers

Figure 27. Zoomed Portion of JPEG Text

This speckled blurring of your information is in all *lossy* compressions.

Tecplot™ and Colors

Tecplot is a wonderful graphic program with lots of features. The 3D flow and temperature fields produced by EFDC and displayed in Figure 2 were created with Tecplot. For Versions 8 and before, Tecplot output graphic animations as Raster Meta (RM) files. The RM format was widely used in early NASA projects. RM files contain only 256 colors and are readily converted to GIFs with lossless compressions, preserving every detail. Version 9 and later outputs AVIs, which have 24-bit (16,777,216) colors and *lossy* compression. Lossless 256-color output is no longer an option. That's why I keep a copy of each (V8 and V9) on two separate machines so that I can still choose.

So how did Tecplot V8 create color depth? Let's see by expanding Figure 2.

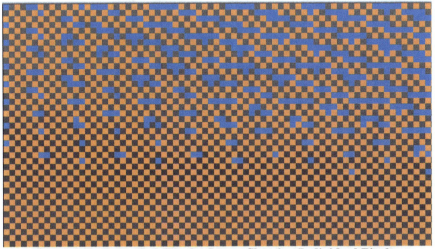

Figure 28. Expanded Tecplot Image Showing Individual Pixels

Different shades of orange are created by surrounding an orange pixel with various shades of gray. The same can be accomplished for all of the main colors using only 16 or 32 shades of gray and still be under the 256 color (1 byte per pixel) requirement. Wikipedia describes this process, "*ordered dithering* is commonly used to display a continuous image on a smaller color depth." Switching frames of an animation back-and-forth between this ordered dithering and 24-bit color depth is impractical because the information available at the time the dithered image was created isn't available for the transformation. Therefore, you must create an animation with the color depth you intend to use. OpenGL does not do 8-bit dithered coloring; so if you want that type of color image in order to create a GIF, you won't be using OpenGL. As it turns out... this is exactly the coloring mode used by TP2 to create 3D images. [There is also a 24-bit color version of TP2 but not all of the features are available.] Let's see how this works out using a familiar figure:

Figure 29. Dithered 3D Image Displayed Using TP2

There are only 33 colors in this image, well below the 256 (1 byte per pixel) limit.

Let's zoom in to see the dithering around the right eye:

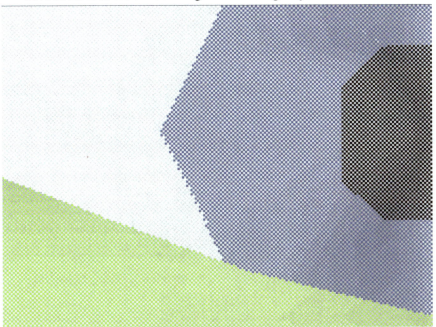

Figure 30. Ordered Dithering

So where is this headed? All of the many transformations, projections, and matrix operations performed by OpenGL in order to render 3D objects are implemented inside TP2 (and were originally implemented in FORTRAN before I converted it all to C). All that effort so that I could render any 3D object using only 256 colors and so deliver those images and animations as GIFs.

Let's see what this same object looks like rendered using OpenGL. You can download free the program and source code for View3D, which utilizes OpenGL in the archive accompanying the 3D rendering series at the website listed beneath the Preface.

Here is the result:

Figure 31. Same Object Rendered with View3D Using OpenGL

This particular image only uses 203 colors. Of course, the source (triangles) only uses 5 (green, red, blue, white, and black). The rest are shades (mostly green and red) based on lighting and shadows. Still, there is more detail. This next figure shows the area around the eye zoomed in:

Figure 32. Zoom Eye Detail

There are only 31 colors in this limited area, which is well within the 256 (1 byte per pixel) limit for a GIF. While this is only one example and the coloring is rather simple, it does raise the question of whether or not 24-bit/pixel color is really worth it. Let's consider a more colorful example.

Figure 33. T-Rex Displayed with View3D Using OpenGL

This image contains 34,826 colors, far more than the 256 limit; but let's take a closer look...

Figure 34. Zoomed Detail of OpenGL Rendering

This zoomed section of the whole has 9,736 colors.

49

Along with the 3D triangular elements, the T-Rex 3D Studio™ (.3ds) model contains a flat (2D) "texture" (a JPEG of the skin, eye, lips, and teeth), which OpenGL "stretches" over the elements using the linear basis function in Equations 11.6 and 11.7 to interpolate the red, green, and blue components. If we import the .3ds file into View3D and then export it as a 3D View (.3dv) file, the average RGB for each triangle is associated with the elements, as the latter format does not handle textures, only individual element colors. We get:

Figure 35. Import .3DS Model/Output .3DV Model

which has only 4401 colors. Paint Shop Pro™ can find the optimal 256:

Figure 36. Optimal 256 Color .3DV Model

50

TP2, however, has a built-in palette consisting of the 16 standard Windows colors plus 32 shades of gray plus 128 colors of the rainbow between blue and red, which works for many things but not T-Rex:

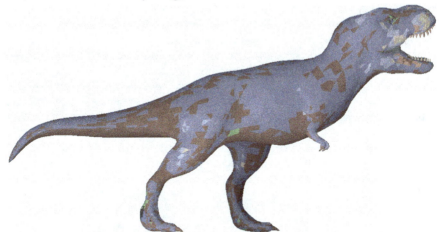

Figure 37. TP2 Limited Coloring of 3DV Model

Only 42 of the total 176 colors are used in this rendering. Some of the matrix operations performed to display this object include:

```
S1=sin(A1);
S2=sin(A2);
S3=sin(A3);
C1=cos(A1);
C2=cos(A2);
C3=cos(A3);
R11=C1*C3-S1*S2*S3;
R12=S1*C3+C1*S2*S3;
R13=-C2*S3;
R21=-S1*C2;
R22=C1*C2;
R23=S2;
R31=-C1*S3-S1*S2*C3;
R32=-S1*S3+C1*S2*C3;
R33=-C2*C3;
for(body=node=0;body<2;body++)
  {
  for(n=0;n<Body.Nn;n++,node++)
    {
    P.x=(Body.Xn[n]-Xc)/Sx;
    P.y=(Body.Yn[n]-Yc)/Sy;
    P.z=(Body.Zn[n]-Zc)/Sz;
    X=R11*P.x+R12*P.y+R13*P.z;
    Y=R21*P.x+R22*P.y+R23*P.z;
    Z=R31*P.x+R32*P.y+R33*P.z;
```

An interesting fact about OpenGL™ is that it only uses floats (32-bit) and not doubles (64-bit) floating-point numbers. When OpenGL was first developed, this was faster but that is no longer the case. OpenGL began on UNIX workstations with different hardware from PCs, which use Intel™. As mentioned previously, Intel's FPUs don't perform 32-bit operations faster than 64-bit or 80-bit. Furthermore, OpenGL transforms most of the 32-bit floating-point operations into scaled 32-bit integer operations with an implied normalizing division, which is not accomplished by the DIV instruction, rather by shifting bits to the right with the ROR (rotate right) instruction, as compared to the SHR (shift right) instruction. The former works for signed integers and the latter for unsigned. This use of integers for many of the matrix options made a huge performance difference in the early days of the PC when OpenGL first appeared there because some machines didn't come with a FPU. OpenGL still works fine on a PC, only there are other implementations of 3D rendering which operate as rapidly.

Chapter 14. Inviscid Flow Example

As mentioned in Chapter 8, Laplace's partial differential equation governs inviscid flow (i.e., negligible viscosity or extremely large Reynolds number). Here we consider an example without all the details usually filling the discussion of partial differential equations, just looking at the array operations and bookkeeping necessary to build such a model. We select a familiar domain for this example—albeit with a little geographic license:

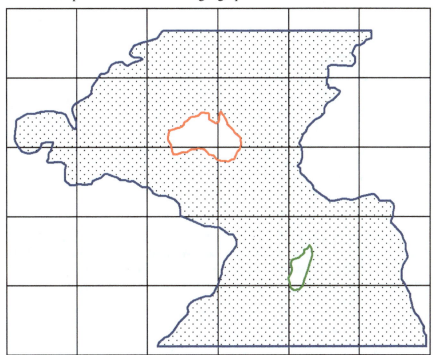

Figure 38. Example Domain for Inviscid Flow

We begin with three polygons:

```
double Coastline[]={3.436,53.517,3.436,51.395,...
  -55.634,53.517,3.436,53.517};
double Australia[]={-38.086,16.265,-38.540,16.070,...
  -38.086,16.265};
double Madagascar[]={-20.206,-17.809,-19.515,...
  19.557,-20.558,-19.879,-19.162,-20.206,-17.809};
```

We fill the domain with evenly-spaced nodes, say 200x200 and allocate some variables:

```
int*flag,i,j,k,nx=200,ny=200;
double*p*x,xm,xx,*y,ym,yx;
flag=calloc(nx*ny,sizeof(int));
x=calloc(nx*ny,sizeof(double));
y=calloc(nx*ny,sizeof(double));
```

We next must find the extent of the domain and fill in arrays x and y:

```
xm=xx=Coastline[0];
ym=yx=Coastline[1];
for(i=2;i<sizeof(Coastline)/sizeof(double)/2;i++)
  {
  if(Coastline[2*i]<xm)
    xm=Coastline[2*i];
  if(Coastline[2*i]>xx)
    xx=Coastline[2*i];
  if(Coastline[2*i+1]<ym)
    ym=Coastline[2*i+1];
  if(Coastline[2*i+1]>yx)
    yx=Coastline[2*i+1];
  }
for(i=0;i<ny;i++)
  {
  for(j=0;j<nx;j++,k++)
    {
    x[k]=xm+j*(xx-xm)/(nx-1);
    y[k]=ym+i*(yx-ym)/(ny-1);
    }
  }
```

Unlike malloc(), the calloc() function initializes the arrays to zero; therefore, all nodes will begin with flag=0. We next assign any node inside the Australia polygon 2, inside the Madagascar polygon 4, and inside the Coastline a value of 1:

```
for(k=0;k<nx*ny;k++)
  {
  if(InsidePolygon(Australia,sizeof(Australia)
    /sizeof(double)/2,x[k],y[k]))
    flag[k]=2;
  else if(InsidePolygon(Madagascar,sizeof(Madagascar)
    /sizeof(double)/2,x[k],y[k]))
    flag[k]=4;
  else if(InsidePolygon(Coastline,sizeof(Coastline)
    /sizeof(double)/2,x[k],y[k]))
    flag[k]=1;
  }
```

We next identify all interior nodes by counting the surrounding nodes whose flag is not zero. Each of these we flag with 8 using the OR (| in C) operation. After this step any node with the 1 bit set is inside the domain, with the 2 bit set is inside Australia, with the 4 bit set is inside Madagascar, and with the 8 bit set is interior.

In order to satisfy Laplace's equation for the interior nodes, all we need to do is average the four surrounding values. The boundary nodes are a little more complicated. We arbitrarily impose a "no flow" condition across the bottom and top. We also impose a lateral flow to the left on the bottom boundary and a lateral flow to the right on the top boundary. To do so, we arbitrarily assign the value of zero to the bottom right node, then increment each node to the left along the bottom boundary by some arbitrary amount, say 1. We continue the final constant value up the Eastern coastline to the top left node. We must then step down to zero across the top boundary, ending at zero at the top right corner. The entire Western boundary is zero, so we don't need to do anything there. As we are setting these boundary nodes, we can also flag them with OR 16 for easy identification.

Interior boundaries are interesting. These are also "no-flow" but we don't know what the value of the potential is at these points. It doesn't matter, so long as it's a constant. We handle this by averaging all the interior nodes surrounding but outside the Australia (2) and Madagascar (4) boundaries and setting the nodes on the boundaries to this average.

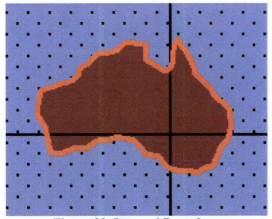

Figure 39. Internal Boundary

To implement the solution we begin by initializing all the interior nodes to some value (it doesn't make much difference what). Then calculate all the interior nodes (averaging the 4 surrounding). Then calculate all the nodes along the Australia and Madagascar boundaries. Because the underlying matrix is diagonally-dominant (like 8.3) this will converge. This yields a regularly-spaced grid containing the resulting potential, which we could display using rainbow colors and contours.

Figure 40. Potential Contours

We can calculate the velocity vectors as in 11.3 by applying the matrix in 11.5.

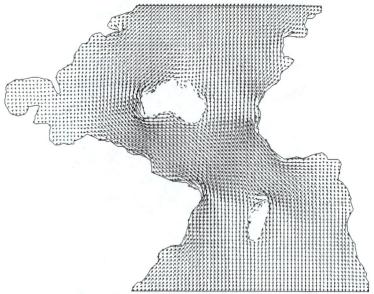

Figure 41. Velocity Vectors

Chapter 15. Steady-State 2D Conduction Using FEM

We have already introduced a basis function (Equation 11.6 and 11.7), which for this problem is: $T(x,y)=a+bx+cy$. We will not go into the details of how we arrive at the equations, which are obtained through the calculus of variations and discussed elsewhere.[14] We will discuss the implementation here, as this is a common example of linear algebra.

We must build the equations one node at a time; however, this will be a sparse matrix—not exactly like 8.3 but similar, only without the obvious structure, as triangular elements can have many arrangements. We know how big the matrices must be because we read in the number of nodes (Nn) and elements (Ne) and thus know the number of unknowns (height) and the nominal terms per unknown (width) of the matrix. We store the index of the three nodes (i, j, and k) in each element in the array Ie[3*ne]. We then calculate the index (Ia) within the A[] matrix of each corresponding term, keeping track of the number of neighboring nodes, which must not exceed some arbitrary limit (Ma) that we can set at the outset:

```
for(i=0;i<Ne;i++)
  {
  for(j=0;j<3;j++)
    {
    n=Ie[3*i+j];
    m=Na[n];
    if(m>=Ma)
      Abort("too many neighbors");
    Ia[Ma*n+m]=i;
    Na[n]++;
    Nt[n]=1;
    }
  }
```

We must count the neighbors:

```
for(i=0;i<Nn;i++)
  {
  memset(Ip,0,Nn*sizeof(int));
  for(j=0;j<Ne;j++)
    {
    l=0;
    for(k=0;k<3;k++)
```

---

[14] Benton, D. James, *Differential Equations: Numerical Methods for Solving*, ISBN-9781983004162, Amazon, 2018.

```
        if(Ie[3*j+k]==i)
          l++;
      if(l==0)
        continue;
      for(k=0;k<3;k++)
        Ip[Ie[3*j+k]]=1;
      }
    n=0;
    for(j=0;j<Nn;j++)
      if(j!=i&&Ip[j]!=0)
        n++;
    Na[i]=n;
    n=0;
    for(j=0;j<Nn;j++)
      if(j!=i&&Ip[j]!=0)
        Ia[Ma*i+n++]=j;
    }
```

The node locations are stored in arrays Xn[] and Yn[]. We then build the nodal point equations:

```
void NodalPointEquations()
  {
  int i,j,n1,n2,n3;
  double AKXY,A11,A12,A13,A22,A23,A33,GA3,
    X1,X12,X13,X2,X23,X3,XY,Y1,Y12,Y13,Y2,Y23,Y3;
  for(i=0;i<Ne;i++) /* element conservation equations */
    {
    n1=Ie[3*i]; /* node 1,2,3 from element Ie[]*/
    n2=Ie[3*i+1];
    n3=Ie[3*i+2];
    X1=Xn[n1]; /* x,y for each node from node[] */
    Y1=Yn[n1];
    X2=Xn[n2];
    Y2=Yn[n2];
    X3=Xn[n3];
    Y3=Yn[n3];
    for(j=0;j<Na[n1];j++) /* index I,J,K from Ia[] */
      Ip[Ia[Ma*n1+j]]=j;
    for(j=0;j<Na[n2];j++)
      Jp[Ia[Ma*n2+j]]=j;
    for(j=0;j<Na[n3];j++)
      Kp[Ia[Ma*n3+j]]=j;
    X12=X2-X1; /* inverse of T(x,y)=a+b*x+c*y */
    X13=X3-X1;
    X23=X3-X2;
    Y12=Y2-Y1;
    Y13=Y3-Y1;
    Y23=Y3-Y2;
    XY=X12*Y23-X23*Y12;
```

58

```
AKXY=Ce[i]*Ae[i]/(XY*XY); /* k*area */
A11= (X23*X23+Y23*Y23)*AKXY;
A12=-(X13*X23+Y13*Y23)*AKXY;
A13= (X12*X23+Y12*Y23)*AKXY;
A22= (X13*X13+Y13*Y13)*AKXY;
A23=-(X12*X13+Y12*Y13)*AKXY;
A33= (X12*X12+Y12*Y12)*AKXY;
Dn[n1]+=A11;
Dn[n2]+=A22;
Dn[n3]+=A33;
An[Ma*n1+Ip[n2]]+=A12; /* left-hand side of A[] */
An[Ma*n1+Ip[n3]]+=A13;
An[Ma*n2+Jp[n1]]+=A12;
An[Ma*n2+Jp[n3]]+=A23;
An[Ma*n3+Kp[n1]]+=A13;
An[Ma*n3+Kp[n2]]+=A23;
GA3=Ge[i]*Ae[i]/3; /* generation term */
Bn[n1]+=GA3; /* right-hand side of A[]X[]=B[] */
Bn[n2]+=GA3;
Bn[n3]+=GA3;
  }
}
```

Notice the similarity of the terms A11, A12, A13, ... to Equation 11.5. We must add the boundary conditions, of which there are 3 types (isothermal, heat flux, and convection):

```
void BoundaryConditions()
  {
  int i,j,j1,j2,k,n,n1,n2;
  double b1,b2,hs,hs3,hs6,hst2,q,s;

  for(n=0;n<Nb;n++)
    {
    i=Ib[n];
    j1=Jb[n];
    j2=(j1+1)%3;
    n1=Ie[3*i+j1];
    n2=Ie[3*i+j2];
    k=Kb[n];
    b1=B1[n];
    b2=B2[n];
    s=Se[3*i+j1];
    if(k==0) /* isothermal */
      {
      Dn[n1]=1;
      Bn[n1]=b1;
      memset(An+Ma*n1,0,Ma*sizeof(double));
      Dn[n2]=1;
      Bn[n2]=b1;
```

```
                memset(An+Ma*n2,0,Ma*sizeof(double));
                }
            else if(k==1) /* heat flux */
                {
                q=b1*s/2;
                Bn[n1]+=q;
                Bn[n2]+=q;
                }
            else /* convection */
                {
                for(j=0;j<Na[n1];j++)
                    Ip[Ia[Ma*n1+j]]=j;
                for(j=0;j<Na[n2];j++)
                    Jp[Ia[Ma*n2+j]]=j;
                hs=b1*s;
                hs3=hs/3;
                hs6=hs/6;
                hst2=hs*b2/2;
                Bn[n1]+=hst2;
                Bn[n2]+=hst2;
                Dn[n1]+=hs3;
                Dn[n2]+=hs3;
                An[Ma*n1+Ip[n2]]+=hs6;
                An[Ma*n2+Jp[n1]]+=hs6;
                }
            }
        }
```

We then solve the system of linear equations using Successive Over-Relaxation because it's easy to implement, works well enough, and the sparseness of the matrix is not a problem. We couldn't vectorize this solution because of the sparseness, which has a different pattern for each problem. The SOR implementation couldn't be any simpler:

```
void SuccessiveOverRelaxation()
    {
    int i,iter,iTx,j;
    double dT,dTx,Told,Tnew;
    for(iter=0;iter<niter;iter++)
        {
        converged=1;
        for(i=0;i<Nn;i++)
            {
            Told=Tn[i];
            Tnew=Bn[i];
            for(j=0;j<Na[i];j++)
                Tnew-=Tn[Ia[Ma*i+j]]*An[Ma*i+j];
            Tnew/=Dn[i];
            Tnew=(1.-Relax)*Told+Relax*Tnew;
            Tn[i]=Tnew;
```

```
         dT=fabs(Tnew-Told);
         if(dT>dTmax)
            converged=0;
      }
   if(converged)
      break;
   }
}
```

We consider a flange, which is divided into 239 triangular elements containing 149 nodes:

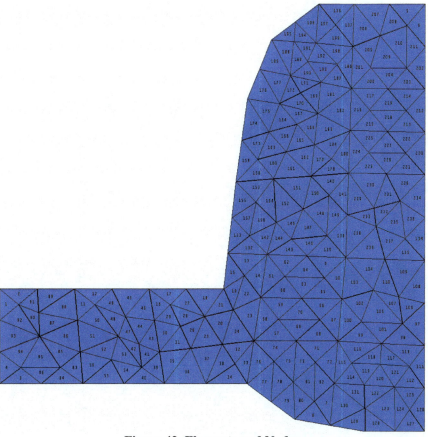

Figure 42. Elements and Nodes

The abbreviated output is shown below:

```
CON2D/V2.11: 2D Finite Element Conduction Model
by Dudley J. Benton, (c)1985-1998
prefix: flange
INPUT FILE: flange.FEM     TITLE: INPUT FILE: FLANGE.P2D
ELEMENTS=239, NODES=142, BOUNDARIES=43
PRINT=1, MAP=1, NITER=100, RELAX=1.5, DTMAX=0.1
ELEM <--- NODE ---> GENERATION CONDUCTIVY       AREA SIDE
   1   36   37   44          1          1     0.0216  BII
   2   37   38   44          1          1     0.0208  BII
   3   33   34   45          1          1    0.02275  BII
BCND ELEM SIDE TYPE     BOUNDARY  CONDITION
   1    5    1 ISOT         700          0
   2    6    1 ISOT         700          0
   3  202    1 ISOT         700          0
  12  127    1 FLUX           0          0
  13  128    1 FLUX           0          0
  14  129    2 FLUX           0          0
  24    4    1 ISOT         100          0
  25   93    1 ISOT         100          0
  26    1    1 ISOT         100          0
  27    2    1 FLUX           0          0
  28   89    2 FLUX           0          0
  29   12    1 FLUX           0          0
NODE NEIGHBORS ->
   1    2   43   55   56   99
   2    1    3   99  112
   3    2    4  111  112  113
   4    3    5  113  116
   5    4    6  116  117
   6    5    7  117  122
   7    6    8  122  127
   8    7    9  127  129
   9    8   10  101  129
  10    9   11  101  102  133
  11   10   12   46  133
  12   11   13   46
  13   12   14   46  132
  14   13   15  130  132  134
  15   14   16  134  135  137
  16   15   17  137  138  140
  17   16   18  100  140
  18   17   19   90   91  100
  19   18   20   86   91
  20   19   21   86   87   92
  21   20   22   92   93   98
  22   21   23   98
  23   22   24   93   97   98
  24   23   25   97
  25   24   26   47   48   97
  26   25   27   48   81
  27   26   28   81   82
  28   27   29   63   67   82
  29   28   30   62   64   67
  30   29   31   64   66   68
```

```
ITER NODE      DTMAX
   1   37    707.143
   2   37    353.571
   3   37    176.786
   4   38    109.665
   5   38     57.3538
   6   38     54.6242
   7   40     25.2103
   8   38     18.8885
   9   40     10.8934
  10   58      7.94229
  40   42      0.152878
  41   42      0.138574
  42   42      0.125721
  43   42      0.114155
  44   42      0.103734
  45   42      0.0943324
BCND ELEM SIDE TYPE  HEAT FLUX
   1    5   1 ISOT    6.19933
   2    6   1 ISOT    7.4392
   3  202   1 ISOT   17.1854
   4  212   1 ISOT   23.8718
   5  220   1 ISOT   32.102
   6  234   2 ISOT   43.4629
   7  134   1 ISOT   53.5591
   8  108   1 ISOT   66.8315
   9   97   1 ISOT   71.2766
  10  111   1 ISOT   74.0438
  11  126   2 ISOT   73.0595
  12  127   1 FLUX          0
  13  128   1 FLUX          0
  14  129   2 FLUX          0
  15    8   1 FLUX          0
  16   79   1 FLUX          0
  17   77   1 FLUX          0
  18   34   2 FLUX          0
  19   36   1 FLUX          0
  20   40   1 FLUX          0
  21   55   2 FLUX          0
  22   84   1 FLUX          0
  23    3   1 FLUX          0
GROSS HEAT FLOW   =    348.698
NET    HEAT FLOW  =    -11.739
TOTAL GENERATION  =      6.95
HEAT IMBALANCE    =     -4.789
plot file: flange.TP2
element file: flange.ELE
temperature file: flange.TRI
```

The calculated temperatures are shown in this next figure:

Figure 43. Calculated Temperatures

Chapter 16. Plane Stress and Strain Using FEM

We next consider a common topic of structural analysis or the calculation of how forces deform objects. For the two-dimensional case we consider those forces per unit area (stress) and resulting deformations (strain) as occurring in a plane. The primary variables are shown in this first figure:

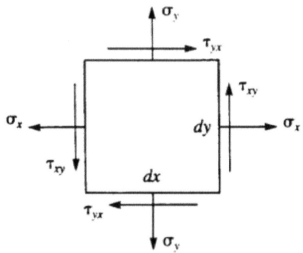

Figure 44. Variables for Plane Stress and Strain

For reasons we won't discuss here, both the stress and strain satisfy Laplace's equation; however, as the two are related (the former causes the latter), the problem we must solve is more like Poisson's equation, making this task a step more complicated to implement than the one in the previous chapter. We can express the problem in matrix form:

$$\begin{Bmatrix} \sigma_x \\ \sigma_y \\ \tau_{xy} \end{Bmatrix} = [D] \begin{Bmatrix} \varepsilon_x \\ \varepsilon_y \\ \gamma_{xy} \end{Bmatrix} \tag{16.1}$$

where the left-hand side is called the *stress tensor* and has three terms: the stress in the x and y directions plus the shear in the xy plane. The matrix **[D]** links the strain to the stress. The far right-hand side is the *strain tensor*, also consisting of three terms: the strain in the x and y directions and the shearing strain associated with the third stress term. For plane stress the matrix [D] is given by:

65

$$[D] = \frac{E}{1-v^2} \begin{bmatrix} 1 & v & 0 \\ v & 1 & 0 \\ 0 & 0 & \dfrac{1-v}{2} \end{bmatrix} \tag{16.2}$$

where E is Young's modulus and v is Poisson's Ratio. For plane strain the matrix [D] is given by:

$$[D] = \frac{E}{(1+v)(1-2v)} \begin{bmatrix} 1-v & v & 0 \\ v & 1-v & 0 \\ 0 & 0 & \dfrac{1}{2}-v \end{bmatrix} \tag{16.3}$$

Because the stress and strain satisfy Laplace's equation, we use the same basis function as before: $f(x,y)=a+bx+cy$. Matrix **[D]** can be programmed using conditional statements:

```
void getD(STIF stif,double ym,double nu,double*D)
   {
   double c;
#if(defined(PlaneStress))
   c=ym/(1.0-nu*nu);
   D[0]=c;
   D[1]=nu*c;
   D[2]=0.;
   D[3]-nu*c;
   D[4]=c;
   D[5]=0.;
   D[6]=0.;
   D[7]=0.;
   D[8]=(1.-nu)*0.5*c;
#elif(defined(PlaneStrain))
   c=ym/((1.+nu)*(1.-2.*nu));
   D[0]=(1.-nu)*c;
   D[1]=nu*c;
   D[2]=0.;
   D[3]=nu*c;
   D[4]=(1.-nu)*c;
   D[5]=0.;
   D[6]=0.;
   D[7]=0.;
   D[8]=(0.5-nu)*c;
#else
   #error neither PlaneStrain nor PlaneStress
#endif
   }
```

66

The stiffness matrix contains many elements similar to the ones in the previous two examples, including the following:

$$[B] = \frac{1}{2A} \begin{bmatrix} y_{23} & 0 & y_{31} & 0 & y_{12} & 0 \\ 0 & x_{32} & 0 & x_{13} & 0 & x_{21} \\ x_{32} & y_{23} & x_{13} & y_{31} & x_{21} & y_{12} \end{bmatrix} \qquad (16.4)$$

where A is the area of the triangular element and just happens to be twice the determinant which appears as Equation 11.5. To facilitate this process, we define a structure for the stiffness matrix:

```
typedef struct{double x13,x1,x21,x23,x2,x32,x3,y12,y13,
   y1,y23,y2,y31,y3;}STIF;
STIF Stiff(double x1,double y1,double x2,double y2,
   double x3,double y3)
   {
   static STIF stif;
   stif.x1=x1;
   stif.y1=y1;
   stif.x2=x2;
   stif.y2=y2;
   stif.x3=x3;
   stif.y3=y3;
   stif.x13=x1-x3;
   stif.x32=x3-x2;
   stif.x21=x2-x1;
   stif.x23=x2-x3;
   stif.y13=y1-y3;
   stif.y23=y2-y3;
   stif.y31=y3-y1;
   stif.y12=y1-y2;
   return(stif);
   }
```

On a programming note, the stiffness matrix must be declared static; because local variables are meaningless (and lost on the stack) when returning from a function such as this. With the stiffness matrix, we can then calculate [B]:

```
void getB(STIF stif,double*B)
   {
   double det;
   det=stif.x13*stif.y23-stif.x23*stif.y13;
   B[ 0]=stif.y23/det;
   B[ 1]=0.;
   B[ 2]=stif.y31/det;
   B[ 3]=0.;
   B[ 4]=stif.y12/det;
   B[ 5]=0.;
   B[ 6]=0.;
```

```
B[ 7]=stif.x32/det;
B[ 8]=0.;
B[ 9]=stif.x13/det;
B[10]=0.;
B[11]=stif.x21/det;
B[12]=stif.x32/det;
B[13]=stif.y23/det;
B[14]=stif.x13/det;
B[15]=stif.y31/det;
B[16]=stif.x21/det;
B[17]=stif.y12/det;
}
```

If you break a program down into individual distinct tasks, as illustrated by these two functions, it is easier to optimize and debug than one long rambling code.

Gauss-Jordan Elimination

In this particular implementation we solve the global matrix for the nodal point displacements using Gauss-Jordan elimination rather than Gauss-Seidel or SOR. One reason is the pattern of sparseness in the matrix eliminates vectorizable options but the primary reason is that the matrix is not always diagonally dominant. The material strength parameters (Young's modulus and Poisson's ratio) can vary considerably, especially when the domain contains multiple materials. The acuteness or obliqueness of the elements as well as the clustering around a single node can result in a problem that won't converge with iterative approaches. Gauss-Jordan is somewhat brute force for this application but works well enough for a few thousand nodes and elements. For very large problems, we are forced to try other options. These can be selected using conditional compilation statements or reading in an optional parameter.

Triangular Elements and Mesh Generation

There are many methods for generating a mesh consisting of triangular elements for any given domain. A search for "Delaunay triangulation" will yield some interesting reading. You may have heard that long thin or short fat triangles are a problem or that a mixture of large and small ones can be a problem. These warnings are valid but there is always the question of, "How much is too much and how little is too little." While there are a few guidelines, this most often takes a guess and several iterations to arrive at a suitable grid. In the case of plane stress or strain, the iteration may be simple. When it comes to CFD, plan to devote more effort to grid refinement.

The following is a triangular mesh surrounding an airfoil at a high angle of attack. Note the smaller elements around the areas of particular interest (leading and trailing edge).

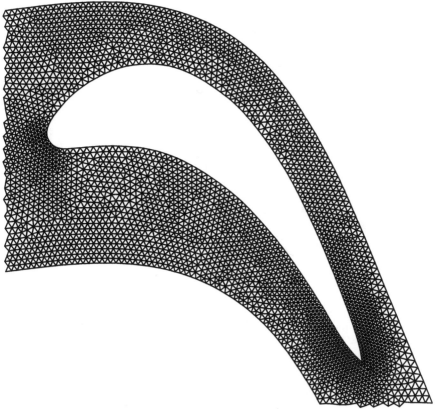

Figure 45. Grid for CFD Modeling

There are many mesh generation tools online, including one (elem3) available free at the website listed beneath the Preface.

We will consider a round object with three round holes for our example of loading and deformation. The basic shape is:

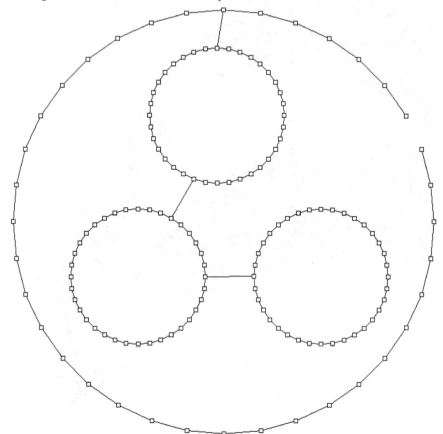

Figure 46. Loaded Object

Next, we fill the domain with triangular elements:

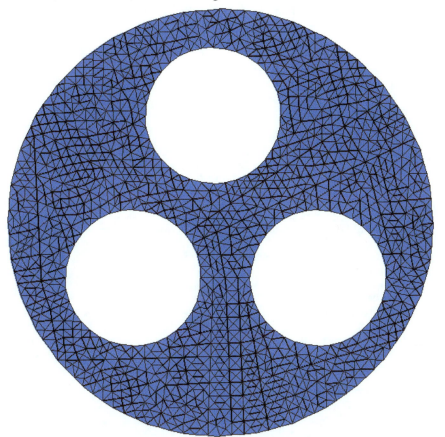

Figure 47. Triangular Elements

The input file looks like this:

```
1376 2540 1 5 <nodes, elements, loads, bearings
9.725 5.952 <X,Y
9.669 6.071
9.613 6.191
...
 21 22 225 20000 0.3 0.1 <nodes, Younge, Poisson, thick
138 21 225 20000 0.3 0.1
 44 45 226 20000 0.3 0.1
21 0 -15 <node, Fx, Fy
190 0 3   <node, Rx, Ry
191 0 3
192 0 3
193 0 3
```

We next run the program:

```
Plane Strain Finite Element Model
reading input: plate.fem
  reading 1376 nodes
  reading 2540 elements
  reading 1 loads
  reading 5 bearings
begin solution
  sizing matrices
  applying point loads
  applying bearings using penalty method
  solving matrix for results
  calculating displacements
saving results: psfem.out
```

The program results are:

```
input file: plate.fem
  nodes=1376
  elements=2540
  point loads=1
  bearings=5
  zoom=5
node deformations
i dx dy
1 0.00393434 -0.00773359
2 0.00266332 -0.00844202
3 0.00132466 -0.00904233
...
-0.0337856<dx<0.0338898
-0.0850667<dy<0.00142301
element stress
i sx sy sxy
1 -576.159 -860.118 -387.211
2 -1003.64 -451.664 -361.093
3 175.638 -47.3432 10.8591
...
-1003.64<sx<713.229
-1086.06<sy<114.963
-387.211<sxy<421.421
element strain
i ex ey exy
1 -0.00944292 -0.0279003 -0.0503375
2 -0.0368581 -0.000979734 -0.0469421
3 0.00891472 -0.00557905 0.00141168
...
-0.0368581<ex<0.0349204
-0.0408012<ey<0.0148648
-0.0503375<exy<0.0547847
```

We load the object by pushing down on the top in the center and supporting it beneath by not allowing the bottom 5 nodes to move vertically, although they can still spread horizontally.

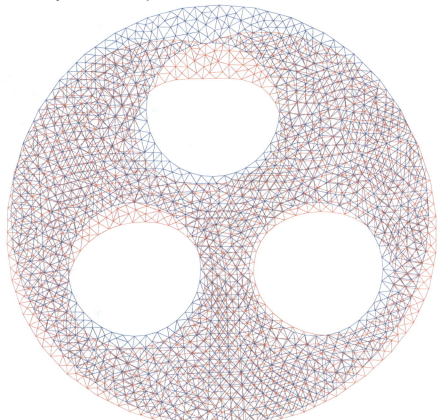

Figure 48. Original (blue) and Deformed (red) Nodes

The node displacement in this figure has been exaggerated by 5x.

The elements are numbered in this zoomed portion:

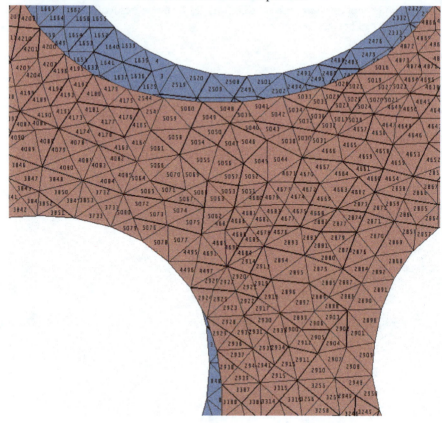

Chapter 17. An Example with History

One of the early applications that became the impetus for many software developments is that of aerodynamics. NASA funded many of these projects, which often taxed or exceeded the computational power available at the time, inspiring various innovations. One such story involves my Boss, who gave me the wonderful opportunity of working at TVA's Engineering Laboratory for 13 years: Dr. William R. Waldrop.

Figure 49. Saturn V Engines

Bill was in the Air Force on loan to Lockheed, overseeing a few projects. At that time, Lockheed was developing the Saturn V rocket for NASA. As part of their contract with NASA, Lockheed promised to deliver a 3D model of the Saturn V engines. NASA was particularly concerned because the five engines blasting away next to each other was a new thing and how this might work was anyone's guess. Blast-Off was approaching and NO model. NASA was insistent and Lockheed was scrambling. In the meeting around the big table there were only glares and shrugs until Bill raised his hand and said, "I'll do it!"

Bill had never created anything like such a model before—nobody had. That's the point. But Bill saw the opportunity and he pounced on it. After reviewing the available models, which were all much too limited, he finally decided to solve the transient Navier-Stokes equation directly. The FORTRAN program was so enormous and so slow that it would not run on the mainframe at Lockheed but it would run on NASA's bigger machine in Huntsville. It bogged their system down so that work came to a halt. At last a deal was struck: Bill could begin work on Friday evening after everyone had left and run all weekend, as long as he was gone before employees arrived on Monday morning. The model obviously did the trick because the Saturn V was a roaring success. But that's not all... The story gets better.

Bill left the Air Force and went to work for Lockheed, but he always wanted to pursue a PhD. LSU would accept him in Mechanical and Aerospace Engineering, so long as he came fully funded. Every idea was rejected. There was no funding to be had. Sorry... As we have already seen, Bill is not easily discouraged. He found a source of funding to study the processes and develop a computer model of the Mississippi river as it flows out of New Orleans into the Gulf of Mexico. M&AE's response was: We don't do that stuff. The Civil Engineering Department's reaction was, "Huh... do what?" And so Bill suggested the plan to the Chemical Engineering Department, which said, "Yes!"

Figure 50. Mouth of the Mississippi

Bill adapted his Saturn V model to handle the Mighty Mississippi! When Bill formed the Team at the TVA Engineering Laboratory of which I was a part, we would tackle anything. What an adventure!

Navier-Stokes

So what are the Navier-Stokes Equations? If we assume gravity is in the down z direction, they can be written:

$$\rho\left(\frac{\partial u}{\partial t}+u\frac{\partial u}{\partial x}+v\frac{\partial u}{\partial y}+w\frac{\partial u}{\partial z}\right)=-\frac{\partial p}{\partial x}+\mu\left(\frac{\partial^2 u}{\partial x^2}+\frac{\partial^2 u}{\partial y^2}+\frac{\partial^2 u}{\partial z^2}\right) \quad (17.1)$$

$$\rho\left(\frac{\partial v}{\partial t}+u\frac{\partial v}{\partial x}+v\frac{\partial v}{\partial y}+w\frac{\partial v}{\partial z}\right)=-\frac{\partial p}{\partial y}+\mu\left(\frac{\partial^2 v}{\partial x^2}+\frac{\partial^2 v}{\partial y^2}+\frac{\partial^2 v}{\partial z^2}\right) \quad (17.2)$$

$$\rho\left(\frac{\partial w}{\partial t}+u\frac{\partial w}{\partial x}+v\frac{\partial w}{\partial y}+w\frac{\partial w}{\partial z}\right)=-\frac{\partial p}{\partial z}+\mu\left(\frac{\partial^2 w}{\partial x^2}+\frac{\partial^2 w}{\partial y^2}+\frac{\partial^2 w}{\partial z^2}\right)-\rho g \quad (17.3)$$

To this we must add the continuity equation:

$$\frac{\partial \rho}{\partial t} + \frac{\partial(\rho u)}{\partial x} + \frac{\partial(\rho v)}{\partial y} + \frac{\partial(\rho w)}{\partial z} = 0 \qquad (17.4)$$

Of course for the Saturn V engines and also the Mississippi River, density will vary with position and time, so will all three velocity components and pressure. How do we solve this? We rearrange everything to put the temporal partial derivatives on one side: $\partial u/\partial t=...$, $\partial v/\partial t=...$, $\partial w/\partial t=...$, $\partial \rho/\partial t=...$ We calculate the spatial partial derivatives using finite differences. We begin with a guess, calculate the time derivatives, take a tiny step, and march forward in time. At least that's the general idea. It's more complicated than that and we will run into some problems, but that's the challenge.

<u>Manageable Grids</u>

So what does this have to do with Linear Algebra? Well, the arrays will be huge and the calculations many; so we must work to keep it as simple as possible. First of all, the grid (or node arrangement) must be simple, which means a rectangle in 2D or a box in 3D. There may be some difference in spacing, but not too much and only in one direction at a time. We might, for example use the grid on the left but not on the right:

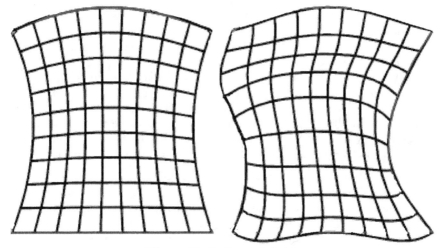

Figure 51. Deformed Grids

Why? Because we want $\partial u/\partial x$ to be $(u[i,j+1]-u[i,j-1])/dx$, accurately enough to yield meaningful results. We don't want to involve 5 or 7 surrounding nodes plus arrays of pointers to element node locations with an entire 4x4 or 5x5 matrix inversion and multiply at each step. We don't want to store all of these intermediate matrices to conserve calculations (seeing as the node x, y, z won't change over time) because we are already consuming a massive amount of memory (certainly in the days of the Saturn V) and don't have room for 16x or 25x more storage.

Time Stepping

Higher order time stepping (e.g., Runge-Kutta) is out of the question because this would require storage of the entire grid of values (ρuvw) at each intermediate step (at least 2x or 4x) in order to implement the algorithm. This leaves two options: Forward Euler or Trapezoidal. Crank-Nicholson is also out of the question because we could never solve such a large set of simultaneous equations. Backward (fully-implicit) Euler is also impractical. What is the problem here? Instability. Experience has proven that while Trapezoidal:

$$u_{t+\Delta t} = u_t + \frac{1}{2}\left[\left(\frac{\partial u}{\partial t}\right)_t + \left(\frac{\partial u}{\partial t}\right)_{t+\Delta t}\right]$$ (17.5)

does provide the advantage of somewhat larger time steps without resulting in instability, the computational burden is not worth it. Specifically, more than twice the computational effort (i.e., quantity of numbers crunched) does not necessarily allow for twice the time step. We are, therefore, stuck with Forward Euler and small time steps.

Before we move on there is another problem with time stepping we must consider. If we merely go through and update the variables (ρuvw) as we compute the partial derivatives, this will produce unwanted *artifacts* in the result. For example, something like a *wave* will appear to form where the calculations begin (i=j=k=0) and move radially outward. This occurs because we are changing the values used to calculate the partial derivatives. In order to eliminate this, we must calculate—but not apply—all of the new values and apply them only after completing the partials. This means 2x storage (old and new). We would have this same problem regardless, so the previous 4x option would actually mean 8x: impossible in the days of the Saturn V and perhaps impractical now for moderately large problems without a super computer.

MacCormack Scheme

The same unwanted artifact problem arises from spatial derivatives of the Navier-Stokes and similar partial differential equations. The problem can be understood in terms of the transmission of information. If something is happening upstream of a node, say a pressure wave is building or turbulence is forming, it arrives downstream over time in the direction of flow. The nodes further downstream of the disturbance are unaware of what is a future event for them. If we include the *informed* and *ignorant* nodes in the partial derivatives, we will be calculating an inaccurate picture of what's happening. This sort of thing occurs because our grid and finite differences are an approximation of the real world and its processes.

The first approach developed to avoid this problem is called *upwind* differencing and is simple enough to implement. Instead of taking a central

78

difference, we take a one-sided difference into the wind, as it were. This works well enough for first-order partial derivatives but what about second-order? We need at least three nodes in a row for that. If these are all on one side or the other of the central node, many unwanted artifacts will appear. In fact, using the customary three-node second-order partial differentials in the spatial directions in aerodynamic or hydrodynamic models will produce a sort of sloshing effect of waves bouncing back-and-forth across the domain, reflecting off the boundaries. So what else can we do?

While working on this problem in the field of aerospace at NASA, MacCormack found a practical solution.[15] If we flip-flop (alternate spatial directions) each time we calculate the spatial partials, this will stop the artificial waves from propagating without significantly diminishing the accuracy of the calculations essential to solving the governing partial differential equation and without adding any other unwanted temporal artifacts. With all of these considerations combined (node arrangement and packing, time stepping, and spatial differentials), we can solve very large problems that were previously considered intractable.

1D Example

The primary focus of the TVA Engineering Laboratory back in the day was the operation and maintenance of the many lakes and hydroelectric dams. Naturally, Dr. Waldrop's experience was put to good use in the computer models used to manage the reservoirs.

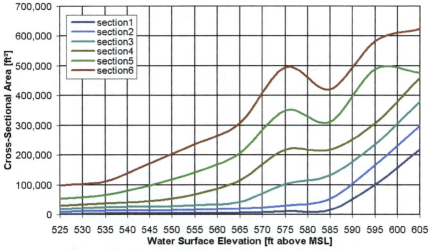

Figure 52. Wheeler Reservoir Cross-Sectional Areas

---

[15] MacCormack, R. W., "The Effect of Viscosity in Hypervelocity Impact Cratering," AIAA Paper 69-354, 1969.

The simplest of these was a 1D transient model for an open channel bounded above and below by a dam. A model was constructed for each of the rivers, taking into account the physical geometry of the shoreline and riverbed. The gates are open and shut each day to control the levels and deliver electricity during times of peak demand. The cross-sectional areas for six positions along Wheeler Reservoir as a function of water surface elevation are shown in the preceding figure and the channel width in the figure below:

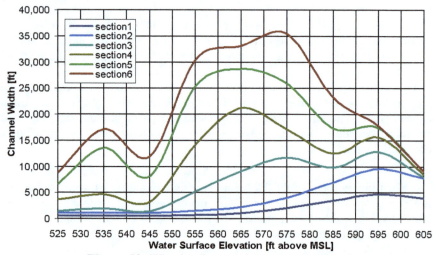

Figure 53. Wheeler Reservoir Channel Widths

The hydraulic radius (raised to the 2/3 power, ready to use) is shown below:

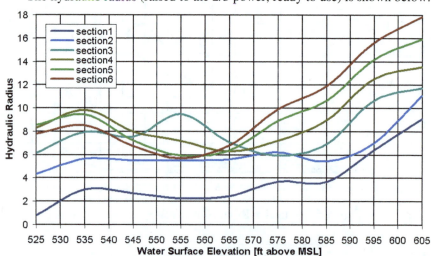

Figure 54. Wheeler Reservoir Hydraulic Radii

80

The spatial derivatives are quite simple (with the flip-flopping MacCormack scheme) and so is the time stepping. We adjust the time step based on many runs until a value is found that satisfies the Courant Condition[16] (below) and produces reliably stable results.

$$\frac{u\Delta t}{\Delta x} \leq 1 \qquad (17.6)$$

After that, it's just read in the dam schedule and crunch the numbers:

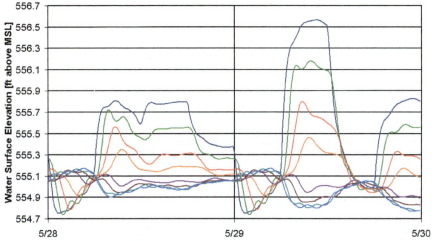

Figure 55. Wheeler Calculated Water Surface Elevations

Significant sloshing and waves do occur, though these would not be obvious to fishermen or boaters, as they are only one or two feet spread out over miles of the river.

[16] Courant, R., Friedrichs, K., and Lewy, H., "On the Partial Difference Equations of Mathematical Physics", *IBM Journal of Research and Development*, Vol. 11, No. 2, pp. 215–234, 1967.

The local transient flow rates are shown in this next figure:

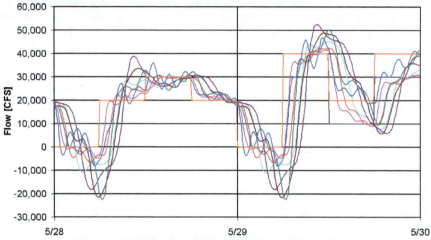

Figure 56. Wheeler Calculated Local Flow Rates

<u>2D Example with Water Quality</u>

While this level of detail (1D flow only) might be adequate for some considerations, it's not enough to analyze and manage an active reservoir home to many living organisms, including fish. For this, we need at least two spatial dimensions and water quality variables, including: temperature, dissolved oxygen, nitrogen, phosphorous, ammonia, algae, and biological oxygen demand (BOD). How do we calculate these things? We stick to the same approach as before: a rectangular grid with the nodes stretched only in one dimension to follow the riverbed. We draw on the many studies of reservoir dynamics and approximations of the processes involved, like oxygen being absorbed at the surface and consumed by organisms. See for example the Wikipedia articles on these subjects. Ultimately, all of these processes can be represented by partial differential equations. These can be rearranged to create the same sort of relationships as for velocity components:

$$\frac{\partial BOD}{\partial t} = \cdots \qquad (17.7)$$

These can all be approximated using finite difference and we can step forward through time, updating all the additional variables using the very same loops. We may have to adjust the time step downward if any of the new processes are occurring rapidly enough to warrant this. What these examples illustrate is that the same approach (node positioning, differential equation rearrangement, slow plug-and-chug time stepping) can work for a variety of problems and can even be run on modest (now old and obsolete) hardware.

82

Typical calculated temperatures are shown in this first figure:

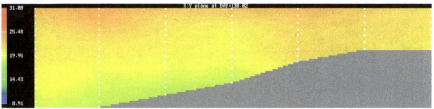

Figure 57. Computed Temperatures

Typical computed dissolved oxygen levels are shown in this next figure:

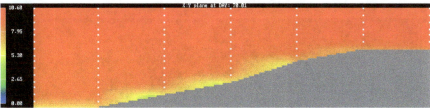

Figure 58. Computed Dissolved Oxygen

In this coloration red is high and blue is low so that this is a good condition. Nitrogen is essential to marine life:

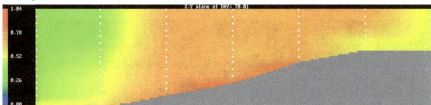

Figure 59. Computed Dissolved Nitrogen

and so is phosphorous:

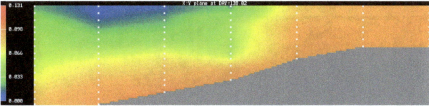

Figure 60. Computed Dissolved Phosphorous

Ammonia is produced by some organisms and consumed by others:

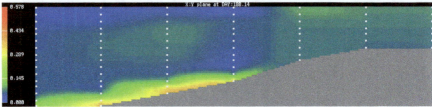

Figure 61. Computed Dissolved Ammonia

Algae grows and shrinks, blooming and dying off with light and other influences. It is also essential to some other organisms.

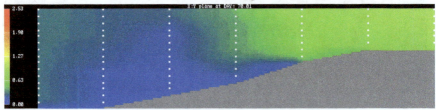

Figure 62. Computed Algae Growth (Change)

The presence of detritus or waste products can consume oxygen and so we calculate this too.

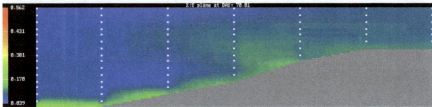

Figure 63. Computed Detritus

The biological oxygen demand considers all of these factors:

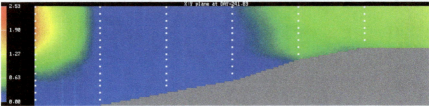

Figure 64. Computed Biological Oxygen Demand

This last result (BOD) is carefully monitored, as it is so important to the health of the marine habitat.

Chapter 18. NAST2D

A similar methodology to the one we have just illustrated has been implemented in the code NAST2D (NAview-STokes 2D), which was originally published in 1998[17] and has gone through several revisions. The code can be found online in several forms, including FORTRAN, C++, and even Python.[18] The code is described as solving the 2D, incompressible Navier-Stokes equations using Chorin's Projection Method[19] for decoupling (a more formal description of what we described in the previous chapter of rearranging the partial differential equations). Some implementations utilize a staggered mesh for spatial discretization, but we will not consider those here; rather, we will be using a regular grid. The Explicit (i.e., Forward) Euler scheme is used for time discretization (viz., exactly what we used in the previous chapter). The implementation we will consider also includes blending of first order upwind and second order central discretization for convective terms, similar to the original MacCormack scheme. SOR is used to solve the Poisson equation (9.1). The pressure update equation is quite simple:

```
for(i=1;i<=imax;i++)
  {
  for(j=1;j<=jmax;j++)
    {
    rhs[i][j]=((f[i][j]-f[i-1][j])/delx
      +(g[i][j]-g[i][j-1])/dely)/delt;
    p[i][j]=(1.-omega)*p[i][j]-beta*((p[i+1][j]
      +p[i-1][j])*rdx2+(p[i][j+1]+p[i][j-1])*rdy2
      -rhs[i][j]);
```

where omega is the relaxation factor (1.7), beta is the Courant ratio, and rdx/2 and rdy/2 are the node spacings. Calculation of the right-hand-side (rhs) includes Δx, Δy, and Δt. The second partials are lengthy but straight-forward:

```
du2dx=((u[i][j]+u[i+1][j])*(u[i][j]+u[i+1][j])
  +fabs(u[i][j]+u[i+1][j])*(u[i][j]-u[i+1][j])
  -(u[i-1][j]+u[i][j])*(u[i-1][j]+u[i][j])
  -fabs(u[i-1][j]+u[i][j])*(u[i-1][j]-u[i][j]))
  /(4.*delx);
```

---

[17] Griebel, M., Dornseifer, T., and Neunhoeffer, T., "Numerical Simulation in Fluid Dynamics," SIAM, 1998.

[18] https://ins.uni-bonn.de/content/software-nast2d

[19] Chorin, A. J., "The Numerical Solution of the Navier-Stokes Equations for an Incompressible Fluid", Bull. Am. Math. Soc., Vol. 73, No. 6, pp. 928–931, 1967.

```
dv2dy=((v[i][j]+v[i][j+1])*(v[i][j]+v[i][j+1])
    +fabs(v[i][j]+v[i][j+1])*(v[i][j]-v[i][j+1])
    -(v[i][j-1]+v[i][j])*(v[i][j-1]+v[i][j])
    -fabs(v[i][j-1]+v[i][j])*(v[i][j-1]-v[i][j]))
    /(4.*dely);
```

Notice that the variables (u, v, p) are arranged on an even grid so that the indexing is simple:

```
u[i][j],u[i+1][j],u[i][j+1],u[i+1][j+1]
```

and the finite difference calculations are also simple. While the equations above might seem a little complicated, the compiler will convert these into very efficient instructions, which can be executed quickly. This is essential to obtaining a solution with lots of nodes and good resolution without requiring too much storage or very long execution times.

This program (NAST2D) is particularly useful for investigating turbulence, as we see in these three figures, which are single frames from an animation representing the time series solution:

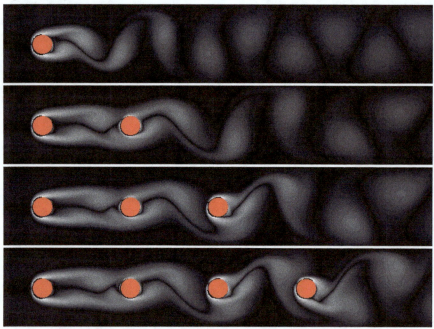

Figure 65. Turbulent Flow Over 1, 2, 3, and 4 Cylinders

86

This next figure shows flow over an ellipse:

Figure 66. Turbulent Flow over an Ellipse

Shapes are easily encoded, such as this airfoil:

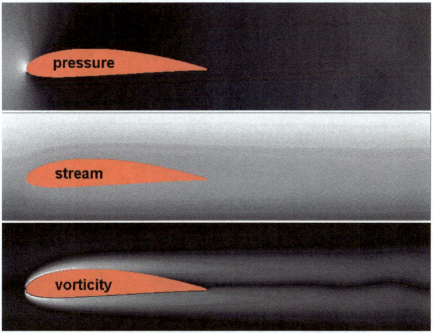

Figure 67. Turbulent Flow over an Airfoil

The implementation which is described elsewhere[20] and available free at the website listed below the Preface can display the results in grayscale or rainbow colors plus show the velocities, pressure, and stream function.

---

[20] Benton, D. James, *Computational Fluid Dynamics: an Overview of Methods*, ISBN-9781672393775, Amazon, 2019.

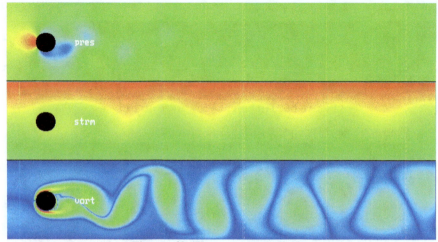

Figure 68. Flow over a Cylinder

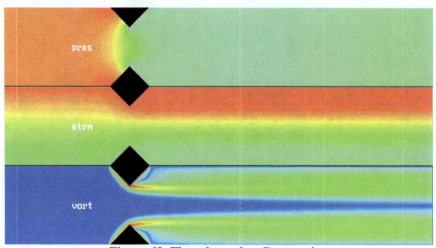

Figure 69. Flow through a Contraction

More examples can be found online and at the website listed beneath the Preface.

Appendix A. Simple Matrix Operation Code

The following C code adds to matrices, which must have the same dimensions:

```c
void MatrixAdd(double*P,double*Q,double*R,int n,int m)
  {
  int i,j;
  for(i=0;i<n;i++)
    for(j=0;j<m;j++)
      R[m*i+j]=P[m*i+j]+Q[m*i+j];
  }
```

A simple change of sign makes this a matrix subtraction:

```c
void MatrixSubtract(double*P,double*Q,double*R,int n,
    int m)
  {
  int i,j;
  for(i=0;i<n;i++)
    for(j=0;j<m;j++)
      R[m*i+j]=P[m*i+j]-Q[m*i+j];
  }
```

The transpose (swap rows and columns) is often needed:

```c
void MatrixTranspose(double*P,double*Q,int n,int m)
  {
  int i,j;
  for(i=0;i<n;i++)
    for(j=0;j<m;j++)
      Q[n*j+i]=P[m*i+j];
  }
```

The determinant can be calculated using Gauss-Jordan elimination down to the point where the matrix is diagonal then returning the product of the diagonal elements, as in this simple code.

```c
double MatrixDeterminant(double*A,int n)
  {
  int i,j,k;
  double d,r;
  for(i=0;i<n;i++)
    {
    if(fabs(A[n*i+i])<FLT_MIN)
      return(0.);
    for(j=i+1;j<n;j++)
      {
```

```
    r=A[n*j+i]/A[n*i+i];
    for(k=0;k<n;k++)
     A[n*j+k]-=r*A[n*i+k];
     }
   }
 for(d=1.,i=0;i< n;i++)
    d*=A[n*i+i];
 return(d);
 }
```

The simplest solution using Gauss-Jordan elimination with row and column pivoting (as discussed previously) is performed by the following, where **AX=B**. The solution is returned in **B** and the matrix **A** is not preserved (i.e., it is altered by this operation).

```
int MatrixSolve(double*A,double*B,int n)
 {
 int i,j,k,ip,jp,*pivot;
 double a,p,b;
 if(n<1)
   return(__LINE__);
 if(n==1)
   {
   a=A[0];
   if(fabs(a)<FLT_MIN)
     return(__LINE__);
   B[0]/=a;
   return(0);
   }
 if((pivot=calloc(n,sizeof(int)))==NULL)
   return(__LINE__);
 for(i=0;i<n;i++)
   pivot[i]=i;
 for(k=0;k<n-1;k++)
   {
   ip=k;
   jp=k;
   p=fabs(A[k*(n+1)]);
   for(i=k;i<n;i++)
     {
     for(j=k;j<n;j++)
       {
       a=fabs(A[n*i+j]);
       if(a>p)
         {
         ip=i;
         jp=j;
         p=a;
         }
       }
     }
```

90

```
      }
   if(p<FLT_MIN)
      {
      free(pivot);
      return(__LINE__);
      }
   if(ip!=k)
      {
      b=B[k];
      B[k]=B[ip];
      B[ip]=b;
      for(j=k;j<n;j++)
         {
         a=A[n*k+j];
         A[n*k+j]=A[n*ip+j];
         A[n*ip+j]=a;
         }
      }
   if(jp!=k)
      {
      j=pivot[jp];
      pivot[jp]=pivot[k];
      pivot[k]=j;
      for(i=0;i<n;i++)
         {
         a=A[n*i+k];
         A[n*i+k]=A[n*i+jp];
         A[n*i+jp]=a;
         }
      }
   for(i=k+1;i<n;i++)
      {
      a=A[n*i+k]/A[n*k+k];
      B[i]-=a*B[k];
      for(j=k+1;j<n;j++)
         A[n*i+j]-=a*A[n*k+j];
      }
   }
a=A[n*n-1];
p=fabs(a);
if(p<FLT_MIN)
   {
   free(pivot);
   return(__LINE__);
   }
B[n-1]/=a;
for(k=1;k<n;k++)
   {
   i=n-1-k;
```

91

```
      b=0.;
      for(j=i+1;j<n;j++)
         b+=A[n*i+j]*B[j];
      B[i]=(B[i]-b)/A[n*i+i];
      }
   for(i=0;i<n;i++)
      A[i]=B[i];
   for(i=0;i<n;i++)
      B[pivot[i]]=A[i];
   free(pivot);
   return(0);
   }
```

In the same way we can add row and column pivoting to the previous function for the determinant. The process is the same as MatrixSolve() except returning the product of the pivot values (without applying fabs() to each one). The simplest algorithm for matrix inversion also utilizes Gauss-Jordan elimination. The inverse is returned in the same location so that **A** is not preserved. This algorithm uses row and column pivoting.

```
int MatrixInvert(double*A,int n)
   {
   int i,*ipivot,j,*jpivot,k;
   double a,p,r;
   if((ipivot=calloc(2*n,sizeof(int)))==NULL)
      return(__LINE__);
   jpivot=ipivot+n;
   for(k=0;k<n;k++)
      {
      ipivot[k]=k;
      jpivot[k]=k;
      p=fabs(A[n*k+k]);
      for(j=k;j<n;j++)
         {
         for(i=k;i<n;i++)
            {
            a=fabs(A[n*j+i]);
            if(a>p)
               {
               p=a;
               ipivot[k]=i;
               jpivot[k]=j;
               }
            }
         }
      if(p<FLT_MIN)
         {
         free(ipivot);
         return(__LINE__);
         }
```

```
        j=ipivot[k];
        if(j!=k)
          {
          for(i=0;i<n;i++)
            {
            a=-A[n*i+k];
            A[n*i+k]=A[n*i+j];
            A[n*i+j]=a;
            }
          }
        i=jpivot[k];
        if(i!=k)
          {
          for(j=0;j<n;j++)
            {
            a=-A[n*k+j];
            A[n*k+j]=A[n*i+j];
            A[n*i+j]=a;
            }
          }
        a=A[n*k+k];
        for(i=0;i<n;i++)
          if(i!=k)
            A[n*k+i]=-A[n*k+i]/a;
        for(i=0;i<n;i++)
          {
          r=A[n*k+i];
          for(j=0;j<n;j++)
            if(i!=k&&j!=k)
              A[n*j+i]+=r*A[n*j+k];
          }
        A[n*k+k]/=a;
        for(j=0;j<n;j++)
          A[n*j+k]/=a;
        }
    for(k=n-2;k>=0;k--)
      {
      i=ipivot[k];
      if(i!=k)
        {
        for(j=0;j<n;j++)
          {
          a=A[n*k+j];
          A[n*k+j]=-A[n*i+j];
          A[n*i+j]=a;
          }
        }
      j=jpivot[k];
      if(j!=k)
```

93

```
    {
    for(i=0;i<n;i++)
      {
      a=A[n*i+k];
      A[n*i+k]=-A[n*i+j];
      A[n*i+j]=a;
      }
    }
  }
free(ipivot);
return(0);
}
```

Appendix B. Accelerated Vector Instructions

Before the explosion of microcomputers, there were mainframes—massive machines filling rooms, consuming lots of power, and requiring devoted cooling equipment. A select few of these had special capabilities, including vector processing: rapidly manipulating arrays of floating-point numbers. Only a dozen or so operations were available (e.g., add, subtract, multiply, divide, etc.) but these simple tasks could be combined to perform larger ones, such as matrix inversion and solution of simultaneous equations. The increase in speed over scalar (many sequential one-at-a-time) operations was achieved using specialized hardware designed specifically for this task.

More recently, some graphic processing units (GPU) "chips" have been utilized to achieve a similar effect. Taking advantage of this computing power requires special hardware and also software, usually in the form of a very expensive compiler. In the early 1980s Hewlett-Packard sold a minicomputer, the HP-1000, that also performed vector instructions very similar to those of the mainframes. They called this "package" of vector instructions the VIS. In 1984 this author created an equivalent set of instructions using assembler that would run on any PC with an Intel™ processor. The instructions include the following:

single	precision	operations	scalar	vector	KFLOP	
kernel	function	[16,128,1024 is the length]	speed	16	128	1024
VABS	abs val	(V2(I)=ABS(V1(I)),I=1,N)	109	14	112	895
VADD	add	(V3(I)=V1(I)+V2(I),I=1,N)	112	14	112	895
VCLA	clamp	(V(I)=VMIN≤V(I)≤VMAX,I=1,N)	224	28	224	1790
VDIV	divide	(V3(I)=V1(I)/V2(I),I=1,N)	112	14	112	895
VDOT	dot prod	S=SUM(V1(I)*V2(I),I=1,N)	112	14	112	895
VMAB	max abs	V(M)=MAX(ABS(V(I)),I=1,N)	112	14	112	895
VMAX	maximum	V(M)=MAX(V(I),I=1,N)	112	14	112	895
VMIB	min abs	V(M)=MIN(ABS(V(I)),I=1,N)	112	14	112	895
VMIN	minimum	V(M)=MIN(V(I),I=1,N)	112	14	112	895
VMOV	move	(V2(I)=V1(I),I=1,N)	112	14	112	895
VMPY	multiply	(V3(I)=V1(I)*V2(I),I=1,N)	112	14	112	895
VNRM	norm	S=SUM(ABS(V1(I)),I=1,N)	112	14	112	895
VPOL	polynomial	P=SUM(C(I)*X**(I-1),I=1,N)	224	28	224	1790
VPIV	pivot	(V3(I)=S*V1(I)+V2(I),I=1,N)	224	28	224	1790
VSAD	add	(V2(I)=S+V1(I),I=1,N)	112	14	112	895
VSDV	divide	(V2(I)=S/V1(I),I=1,N)	112	14	112	895
VSMY	multiply	(V2(I)=S*V1(I),I=1,N)	112	14	112	895
VSSB	subtract	(V2(I)=S-V1(I),I=1,N)	112	14	112	895
VSUB	subtract	(V3(I)=V1(I)-V2(I),I=1,N)	112	14	112	895
VSUM	sum	S=SUM(V1(I),I=1,N)	112	14	112	895
VSWP	swap	(V1(I)<->V2(I),I=1,N)	112	14	112	895
VMIX	index mov	(V2(I)=V1(INDEX(I)),I=1,N)	112	14	112	895
VMXI	index mov	(V2(INDEX(I))=V1(I),I=1,N)	112	14	112	895

These are available free on the Web at the address beneath the Preface. More details can be found in this book, which is available from Amazon:

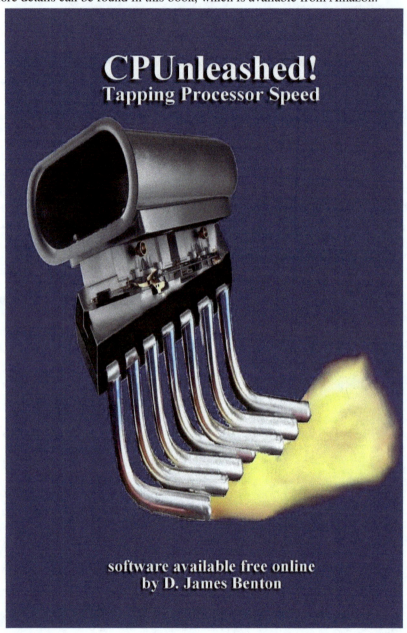

Appendix C. Burkardt's Eispack

John Burkardt is a mathematician and Google Scholar who has taught at several universities, published many papers, and provides a lot of excellent free software. His latest page is:

https://people.sc.fsu.edu/~jburkardt/

One of the items you will find at this site is the eispack, which is a C library that calculates the eigenvalues and eigenvectors of a matrix. This library is also available in FORTRAN, which some may prefer. The library includes the following functions:

BAKVEC .... determines eigenvectors by reversing the FIGI transformation.

BALBAK .... determines eigenvectors by undoing the BALANC transformation.

BANDR.......... reduces a symmetric band matrix to symmetric tridiagonal form.

CBABK2........ finds eigenvectors by undoing the CBAL transformation.

CDIV .... emulates complex division, using real arithmetic.

COMBAK ...... determines eigenvectors by undoing the COMHES transformation.

CSROOT........ computes the complex square root of a complex quantity.

ELMBAK....... determines eigenvectors by undoing the ELMHES transformation.

I4_MAX......... returns the maximum of two I4's.

I4_MIN........... returns the smaller of two I4's.

PYTHAG........ computes SQRT (A * A + B * B) carefully.

R8_EPSILON. returns the R8 round off unit.

R8_MAX........ returns the maximum of two R8's.

R8_MIN .... returns the minimum of two R8's.

R8_SIGN........ returns the sign of an R8.

R8MAT_IDENTITY.....sets an R8MAT to the identity matrix.

R8MAT_MM_NEW .....multiplies two matrices.

REBAK .... determines eigenvectors by undoing the REDUC transformation.

REBAKB........ determines eigenvectors by undoing the REDUC2 transformation.

REDUC .... reduces the eigenvalue problem A*x=lambda*B*x to A*x=lambda*x.

REDUC2 .... reduces the eigenvalue problem A*B*x=lamdba*x to A*x=lambda*x.

97

RS ... computes eigenvalues and eigenvectors of real symmetric matrix.

RSB .. computes eigenvalues and eigenvectors of a real symmetric band matrix.

RSG .. computes eigenvalues/vectors, A*x=lambda*B*x, A symmetric, B pos-def.

RSGAB .... computes eigenvalues/vectors, A*B*x=lambda*x, A symmetric, B pos-def.

RSGBA .... computes eigenvalues/vectors, B*A*x=lambda*x, A symmetric, B pos-def.

RSP... computes eigenvalues and eigenvectors of real symmetric packed matrix.

TIMESTAMP. prints the current YMDHMS date as a time stamp.

TQL2 .... computes all eigenvalues/vectors, real symmetric tridiagonal matrix.

TQLRAT .... computes all eigenvalues of a real symmetric tridiagonal matrix.

TRBAK1 .... determines eigenvectors by undoing the TRED1 transformation.

TRBAK3 .... determines eigenvectors by undoing the TRED3 transformation.

TRED1 .... transforms a real symmetric matrix to symmetric tridiagonal form.

TRED2 .... transforms a real symmetric matrix to symmetric tridiagonal form.

TRED3 .... transform real symmetric packed matrix to symmetric tridiagonal form.

Appendix D. EFDC Solvers

As mentioned in Chapter 9 and illustrated in Figure 2 on page iv, John Hamrick's Environmental Fluid Dynamics Code (EFDC) involves the solution of many equations basically having the form of Poisson's partial differential. During the process of optimization five algorithms were considered: Jacobi, Gauss Seidel, Successive Over-Relaxation, Gram-Schmidt, and Conjugate Gradient. All of these are implemented in one code for comparison, not solving the full model equations, but ones typical of the usual practice. The code (SOLVER.FOR) can be found in the online archive. Abbreviated output of the test is listed here for illustration and comparison of the techniques:

```
THIS PROGRAM ILLUSTRATES THE USE OF THE SEVERAL
MATRIX SOLUTION ALGORITHMS WHICH COULD BE USED FOR
SOLVING THE EXTERNAL MODE EQUATIONS FOR HEAD
INSIDE EFDC. THE CONJUGATE GRADIENT IS USED NOW.
THE MATRIX COEFFICIENTS, INITIAL ESTIMATE, AND FINAL
RESULTS ARE ALL TAKEN FROM AN ACTUAL EFDC MODEL RUN
FOR AN 11 BY 7 GRID.
THE CONJUGATE GRADIENT SUBROUTINE IS TAKEN DIRECTLY
OUT OF EFDC WITH A FEW MODIFICATIONS TO BRING IT UP
TO FORTRAN 90.
MATRIX TO BE SOLVED AND INITIAL ESTIMATE OF SOLUTION
 L SOLUTION  CENTRAL    NORTH     SOUTH      EAST      WEST  RIGHTSIDE
 1 ********   1.00000   0.00000   0.00000   0.00000   0.00000   0.00000
 2 16.28906   1.02821  -0.24883   0.00000  -0.01245   0.00000  12.52400
 3 13.75732   1.00179  -0.21096   0.00000  -0.01145  -0.01245  10.52795
 4 13.00079   1.00000  -0.21013   0.00000  -0.01149  -0.01145   9.96835
 5 12.44556   1.00225  -0.21225   0.00000  -0.01159  -0.01149   9.54457
 6 11.91513   1.00360  -0.21346   0.00000  -0.01162  -0.01159   9.13802
 7 11.37992   1.00458  -0.21370   0.00000  -0.01233  -0.01162   8.71233
 8 12.12990   1.02094  -0.24168   0.00000   0.00000  -0.01233   9.31073
 9 16.28907   1.27703  -0.24883  -0.24883  -0.01245   0.00000  12.52402
10 13.75733   1.21275  -0.21096  -0.21096  -0.01145  -0.01245  10.52798
JACOBI ALGORITHM (INATELY VECTORIZABLE)
 ITER RESIDUAL    TARGET
    1  7.01E+01  1.00E-16
    2  3.79E+00  1.00E-16
    3  3.35E-01  1.00E-16
    4  2.90E-02  1.00E-16
    5  2.61E-03  1.00E-16
    6  2.30E-04  1.00E-16
    7  2.10E-05  1.00E-16
    8  1.88E-06  1.00E-16
    9  1.73E-07  1.00E-16
   23  1.45E-11  1.00E-16
EXTERNAL SOLUTION DID NOT CONVERGE
GAUSS-SEIDEL ALGORITHM (NOT VECTORIZABLE)
```

```
ITER RESIDUAL   TARGET
   1  7.01E+01  1.00E-16
   2  2.92E+00  1.00E-16
   3  8.97E-02  1.00E-16
   4  8.35E-04  1.00E-16
   5  7.33E-06  1.00E-16
   6  6.39E-08  1.00E-16
   7  5.50E-10  1.00E-16
   8  7.89E-12  1.00E-16
   9  2.74E-12  1.00E-16
  23  2.74E-12  1.00E-16
EXTERNAL SOLUTION DID NOT CONVERGE
SUCCESSIVE OVER-RELAXATION (NOT VECTORIZABLE)
ITER RESIDUAL   TARGET
   1  7.01E+01  1.00E-16
   2  1.79E+01  1.00E-16
   3  5.93E+00  1.00E-16
   4  2.20E+00  1.00E-16
   5  8.01E-01  1.00E-16
   6  2.66E-01  1.00E-16
   7  7.87E-02  1.00E-16
   8  2.05E-02  1.00E-16
   9  4.76E-03  1.00E-16
  23  6.77E-11  1.00E-16
EXTERNAL SOLUTION DID NOT CONVERGE
CONJUGATE GRADIENT ALGORITHM (VECTORIZABLE)
(THIS IS THE ALGORITHM UTILIZED BY EFDC)
ITER RESIDUAL   TARGET
   1  1.94E+00  1.00E-16
   2  5.19E-03  1.00E-16
   3  2.61E-04  1.00E-16
   4  2.43E-06  1.00E-16
   5  4.40E-08  1.00E-16
   6  1.12E-09  1.00E-16
   7  3.43E-12  1.00E-16
   8  9.62E-14  1.00E-16
   9  3.10E-15  1.00E-16
  10  1.79E-17  1.00E-16
EXTERNAL SOLUTION CONVERGED
```

also by D. James Benton

3D Articulation: Using OpenGL, ISBN-9798596362480, Amazon, 2021 (book 3 in the 3D series).

3D Models in Motion Using OpenGL, ISBN-9798652987701, Amazon, 2020 (book 2 in the 3D series.

3D Rendering in Windows: How to display three-dimensional objects in Windows with and without OpenGL, ISBN-9781520339610, Amazon, 2016 (book 1 in the 3D series).

A Synergy of Short Stories: The whole may be greater than the sum of the parts, ISBN-9781520340319, Amazon, 2016.

Azeotropes: Behavior and Application, ISBN-9798609748997, Amazon, 2020.

bat-Elohim: Book 3 in the Little Star Trilogy, ISBN-9781686148682, Amazon, 2019.

Boilers: Performance and Testing, ISBN: 9798789062517, Amazon 2021.

Combined 3D Rendering Series: 3D Rendering in Windows®, 3D Models in Motion, and 3D Articulation, ISBN-9798484417032, Amazon, 2021.

Complex Variables: Practical Applications, ISBN-9781794250437, Amazon, 2019.

Compression & Encryption: Algorithms & Software, ISBN-9781081008826, Amazon, 2019.

Computational Fluid Dynamics: an Overview of Methods, ISBN-9781672393775, Amazon, 2019.

Computer Simulation of Power Systems: Programming Strategies and Practical Examples, ISBN-9781696218184, Amazon, 2019.

Contaminant Transport: A Numerical Approach, ISBN-9798461733216, Amazon, 2021.

CPUnleashed! Tapping Processor Speed, ISBN-9798421420361, Amazon, 2022.

Curve-Fitting: The Science and Art of Approximation, ISBN-9781520339542, Amazon, 2016.

Death by Tie: It was the best of ties. It was the worst of ties. It's what got him killed., ISBN-9798398745931, Amazon, 2023.

Differential Equations: Numerical Methods for Solving, ISBN-9781983004162, Amazon, 2018.

Equations of State: A Graphical Comparison, ISBN-9798843139520, Amazon, 2022.

Evaporative Cooling: The Science of Beating the Heat, ISBN-9781520913346, Amazon, 2017.

Forecasting: Extrapolation and Projection, ISBN-9798394019494, Amazon 2023.

Heat Engines: Thermodynamics, Cycles, & Performance Curves, ISBN-9798486886836, Amazon, 2021.

Heat Exchangers: Performance Prediction & Evaluation, ISBN-9781973589327, Amazon, 2017.

Heat Recovery Steam Generators: Thermal Design and Testing, ISBN-9781691029365, Amazon, 2019.

Heat Transfer: Heat Exchangers, Heat Recovery Steam Generators, & Cooling Towers, ISBN-9798487417831, Amazon, 2021.

Heat Transfer Examples: Practical Problems Solved, ISBN-9798390610763, Amazon, 2023.

The Kick-Start Murders: Visualize revenge, ISBN-9798759083375, Amazon, 2021.

Jamie2: Innocence is easily lost and cannot be restored, ISBN-9781520339375, Amazon, 2016-18.

Kyle Cooper Mysteries: Kick Start, Monte Carlo, and Waterfront Murders, ISBN-9798829365943, Amazon, 2022.

The Last Seraph: Sequel to Little Star, ISBN-9781726802253, Amazon, 2018.

Little Star: God doesn't do things the way we expect Him to. He's better than that! ISBN-9781520338903, Amazon, 2015-17.

Living Math: Seeing mathematics in every day life (and appreciating it more too), ISBN-9781520336992, Amazon, 2016.

Lost Cause: If only history could be changed..., ISBN-9781521173770, Amazon, 2017.

Mass Transfer: Diffusion & Convection, ISBN-9798702403106, Amazon, 2021.

Mill Town Destiny: The Hand of Providence brought them together to rescue the mill, the town, and each other, ISBN-9781520864679, Amazon, 2017.

Monte Carlo Murders: Who Killed Who and Why, ISBN-9798829341848, Amazon, 2022.

Monte Carlo Simulation: The Art of Random Process Characterization, ISBN-9781980577874, Amazon, 2018.

Nonlinear Equations: Numerical Methods for Solving, ISBN-9781717767318, Amazon, 2018.

Numerical Calculus: Differentiation and Integration, ISBN-9781980680901, Amazon, 2018.

Numerical Methods: Nonlinear Equations, Numerical Calculus, & Differential Equations, ISBN-9798486246845, Amazon, 2021.

Orthogonal Functions: The Many Uses of, ISBN-9781719876162, Amazon, 2018.

Overwhelming Evidence: A Pilgrimage, ISBN-9798515642211, Amazon, 2021.

Particle Tracking: Computational Strategies and Diverse Examples, ISBN-9781692512651, Amazon, 2019.

Plumes: Delineation & Transport, ISBN-9781702292771, Amazon, 2019.

Power Plant Performance Curves: for Testing and Dispatch, ISBN-9798640192698, Amazon, 2020.

Props, Fans, & Pumps: Design & Performance, ISBN-9798645391195, Amazon, 2020.

Remediation: Contaminant Transport, Particle Tracking, & Plumes, ISBN-9798485651190, Amazon, 2021.

ROFL: Rolling on the Floor Laughing, ISBN-9781973300007, Amazon, 2017.

Seminole Rain: You don't choose destiny. It chooses you, ISBN-9798668502196, Amazon, 2020.

Septillionth: 1 in 10^{24}, ISBN-9798410762472, Amazon, 2022.

Software Development: Targeted Applications, ISBN-9798850653989, Amazon, 2023.

Software Recipes: Proven Tools, ISBN-9798815229556, Amazon, 2022.

Steam 2020: to 150 GPa and 6000 K, ISBN-9798634643830, Amazon, 2020.

Thermochemical Reactions: Numerical Solutions, ISBN-9781073417872, Amazon, 2019.

Thermodynamic and Transport Properties of Fluids, ISBN-9781092120845, Amazon, 2019.

Thermodynamic Cycles: Effective Modeling Strategies for Software Development, ISBN-9781070934372, Amazon, 2019.

Thermodynamics - Theory & Practice: The science of energy and power, ISBN-9781520339795, Amazon, 2016.

Version-Independent Programming: Code Development Guidelines for the Windows® Operating System, ISBN-9781520339146, Amazon, 2016.

The Waterfront Murders: As you sow, so shall you reap, ISBN-9798611314500, Amazon, 2020.